WARRIOR • 160

DESERT RAT 1940–43

British and Commonwealth troops in North Africa

TIM MOREMAN

ILLUSTRATED BY STEVE NOON

Series editor Marcus Cowper

First published in Great Britain in 2011 by Osprey Publishing
PO Box 883, Oxford, OX1 9PL, UK
PO Box 3985, New York, NY 10185-3985, USA
E-mail: info@ospreypublishing.com

Osprey Publishing, part of Bloomsbury Publishing Plc

Transferred to digital print on demand 2015.

First published 2011
2nd impression 2012

Printed and bound by PrintOnDemand-Worldwide.com,
Peterborough, UK.

A CIP catalogue record for this book is available from the
British Library.

ISBN: 978 1 84908 501 4
PDF e-book ISBN: 978 1 84908 502 1
EPUB e-book ISBN: 978 1 84908 905 0

Editorial by Ilios Publishing Ltd, Oxford, UK
   (www.iliospublishing.com)
Page layout by Mark Holt
Index by Sandra Shotter
Typeset in Sabon and Myriad Pro
Originated by Blenheim Colour

The Woodland Trust
Osprey Publishing are supporting the Woodland Trust, the
UK's leading woodland conservation charity, by funding the
dedication of trees.

www.ospreypublishing.com

Artist's note
Readers may care to note that the original paintings from which
the colour plates in this book were prepared are available for private
sale. All reproduction copyright whatsoever is retained by the
Publishers. All enquiries should be addressed to:
Steve Noon,
50 Colchester Avenue,
Penylan,
Cardiff,
CF23 9BP,
UK
The Publishers regret that they can enter into no correspondence
upon this matter.

Back-cover photographs
Imperial War Museum, E6377 and CBM1358.

The Imperial War Museum collections
The photos in this book come from the Imperial War Museum's
huge collections, which cover all aspects of conflict involving Britain
and the Commonwealth since the start of the 20th century. These
rich resources are available online to search, browse and buy at
www.iwmcollections.org.uk. In addition to Collections Online, you
can visit the Visitor Rooms where you can explore over 8 million
photographs, thousands of hours of moving images, the largest
sound archive of its kind in the world, thousands of diaries and
letters written by people in wartime, and a huge reference library.
To make an appointment, call (020) 7416 5320, or
e-mail mail@iwm.org.uk.
Imperial War Museum www.iwm.org.uk

Measurement conversions
Imperial measurements are used almost exclusively throughout this
book. The exception is weapon calibers, which are given in their
official designation, whether metric or imperial. The following data
will help in converting the imperial measurements to metric.

1 mile = 1.6km
1lb = 0.45kg
1oz = 28g
1 yard = 0.9m
1ft = 0.3m
1in. = 2.54cm/25.4mm
1 gal = 4.5 litres
1pt = 0.47 litres
1 ton (US) = 0.9 tonnes
1hp = 0.745kW

CONTENTS

DESERT RAT 1940–43

INTRODUCTION

The iconic nickname of the 'Desert Rats' was initially proudly borne by the officers, NCOs and men of the 7th Armoured Division, who played a central role in winning the high-intensity war of manoeuvre that raged back and forth across the vast, scorching hot and empty deserts of North Africa from its outset until May 1943. This famous formation was formed on 16 February 1940 from units of the Mobile Division (later renamed the 7th Armoured Division) on garrison duty in Egypt. It initially distinguished itself during the defeat of the ill-fated Italian 10th Army at Beda Fomm in what was dubbed the Western Desert and went on to fight in most of the major battles of the North African campaign. Its nickname originated from the emblem proudly displayed on the divisional commander's flag, vehicles and topee flashes depicting a rampant jerboa (a small, fast-moving and hardy desert rodent) on a circular white background atop a red square. This patch was originally designed by the wife of Major-General Michael O'Moore Creagh, the divisional commander, who had sketched a jerboa in Cairo zoo and whose design was finalized by Trooper Ken Hill of the 5th Royal Tank Regiment. A shoulder flash for all members of the division bearing this modified insignia was produced in mid-1943.

The absence of cover in the flat and open desert made it of vital tactical importance. The protection and concealment offered by the slightest undulation in the ground could save a man's life. Destroyed vehicles and patches of rock and scrub could also provide a place of relative safety. (E16691)

The use of the 'Desert Rats' nickname was quickly and quite inaccurately widened, with the British press and public applying it to all British Commonwealth troops who fought as part of Western Desert Force (WDF) and later as Eighth Army. This disparate desert army shared a common experience of fighting in this remote and exotic theatre of war, which for a long time was the only place where British forces could strike back against the Axis powers on land.

Indeed, the nickname has become part of the distinctive corporate identity of Eighth Army. This book adopts the wider definition of the name by viewing the Desert Rats as, in Churchill's words, 'all those who marched and fought in the Desert Army'.

CHRONOLOGY

1940

10 June	Italy declares war on France and Great Britain.
24 June	France signs armistice with Italy.
28 June	Rudolfo Graziani appointed as Italian commander in Libya.
13 September	Italians invade Egypt, capturing Sollum.
16 September	Italians occupy Sidi Barrani.
8 December	Operation *Compass* begins.
10 December	Sidi Barrani recaptured.
12 December	The 7th Armoured Division arrives at Buq Buq.
17 December	Sollum reoccupied.
24 December	Bardia invested.

1941

3–5 January	The 6th Australian Division captures Bardia; 40,000 prisoners of war are captured.
21–22 January	The 6th Australian Division captures Tobruk.
5 February	The 7th Armoured Division establishes a roadblock at Beda Fomm.
7 February	The Italian 10th Army surrenders.
12 February	Generalleutnant Erwin Rommel lands at Tripoli.
20 February	British and German patrols make contact.

5 March	First British troops sail for Greece.
30–31 March	German offensive in Cyrenaica begins.
10 April	Advance elements of Afrika Korps besiege Tobruk.
27 April	Halfaya Pass occupied and British retire into Egypt.
15–17 May	Operation *Brevity* on the Libyan–Egyptian frontier.
15 June	Operation *Battleaxe* launched to relieve Tobruk.
5 July	General Sir Claude Auchinleck replaces Wavell as Commander-in-Chief, Middle East.
18 November	Operation *Crusader* begins, intended to defeat Axis forces in Cyrenaica and relieve Tobruk.
23 November	Auchinleck takes direct control of Eighth Army.
8 December	Rommel decides to withdraw from the *Crusader* battle in order to avoid destruction.
10 December	Tobruk is relieved.
28–30 December	German counter-attack inflicts rebuff on British vanguard.

1942

21 January	German second offensive at El Agheila begins and achieves immediate success.
7 February	Axis advance halted at the Gazala Line.
26 May	Germans attack the Gazala Line, which is quickly outflanked.
30 May	German armour withdraws into the Cauldron.
5 June	Eighth Army launches attack on the Cauldron.
13 June	British withdraw from Gazala defences.
20 June	Germans launch attack on Tobruk.
21 June	Tobruk garrison surrenders; 30,000 prisoners of war are taken along with vast dumps of supplies.
25 June	Lieutenant-General Ritchie is relieved of his command by Auchinleck, who takes direct control of the battle.
28 June	Germans capture Mersa Matruh.

1 July	Eighth Army makes a stand at El Alamein (first battle of El Alamein).
22 July	German forces break off the battle.
13 August	Lieutenant-General Bernard Law Montgomery assumes command of Eighth Army and General Alexander becomes Commander-in-Chief, Middle East.
30 August	Axis forces make last attempt to break through at Alam Halfa.
6 September	Germans retire to start line.
23 October	Second battle of El Alamein begins and rapidly becomes an attritional struggle.
1–2 November	Eighth Army begins Operation *Supercharge* and overwhelms the German defences.
8 November	Operation *Torch* begins in North Africa.
11 November	British units reach the Libyan border.
13 November	Rommel withdraws from El Agheila.
25 December	Eighth Army occupies Sirte.

1943

23 January	Eighth Army enters Tripoli.
4 February	Advance units of Eighth Army cross into Tunisia.
20 March	Eighth Army assaults the Mareth Line.
5–6 April	Battle of Wadi Akarit.
12–13 May	Axis forces in North Africa surrender.

RECRUITING THE DESERT RATS

Those troops who fought under British Command in North Africa came from all over the far-flung British Empire. Indeed, it was a tribute to pre-war planning that troops from such different backgrounds fought successfully alongside each other with minimal difficulty. These men were joined by various smaller Allied contingents – Free French, Polish and Greek – that had escaped the wreck of earlier defeats. From a small beginning the overall size of the British contingent in North Africa steadily increased as the North African campaign progressed, with the make-up of the army constantly changing as a result of battle casualties, large-scale surrender and transfers of formations to other theatres of war.

The mainstay of the army from the outset were British Army units and formations, with representatives of nearly all of its disparate regiments, corps and services participating in the North African campaign. Apart from armoured-car regiments, it enjoyed a virtual monopoly on armoured units that bore the brunt of the North African campaign, with its tanks in either the Royal Tank Regiment (RTR) or former cavalry regiments. The senior command and staff were dominated by British service officers, although a growing number of Indian Army officers also served, particularly following the appointment of General Sir Claude Auchinleck as Commander-in-Chief, Middle East, in July 1941.

The initial quality of British forces in the Western Desert was high. The 'original' British Desert Rats were the men of the 7th Armoured Division, all highly trained long-service pre-war British regulars, most of whom had been on garrison duty in Egypt before World War II began. Although its strength had been augmented by June 1940 by a leavening of individual replacements or reservists from the UK, it was arguably the mostly highly trained formation at the disposal of the British high command after Dunkirk. These hard-bitten British troops performed extremely well during the initial North African campaigns.

Unfortunately, the overall quality of British Army units changed materially for the worse as it underwent massive expansion from its small pre-war size, with a corresponding short-term fall in its quality and overall combat effectiveness. As a result, the ordinary British Desert Rat by mid-1941 was very different from those that had fought in 1940, with the vast majority being citizen-soldiers who had enlisted for the duration of the war. The army was steadily reinforced by part-time Territorial Army soldiers, volunteers and wartime conscripts, either as individual replacements for existing units or else organized into completely new units and formations. The quality of existing formations in theatre fell, moreover, as the initial pool of veteran, highly trained and experienced officers, NCOs and men was progressively diluted as casualties mounted and both personnel, units and complete brigades were transferred elsewhere to spread their experience or to shore up units in other theatres of war.

The vast majority of these 'hostilities only' officers, NCOs and men were brave, determined and had great potential, but they also had much to learn, and to a varying degree these new recruits were not as highly motivated as the regulars. Indeed, the obvious shortcomings of this citizen army's morale and training imposed strict limitations on how Auchinleck handled Eighth Army in battle from July 1941 onwards and, later, on how Montgomery fought his new command at El Alamein, well aware that training standards were low and that wartime British troops had to be carefully managed to sustain morale.

The initial desert veterans of the 7th Armoured Division were joined by significant numbers of troops of very different backgrounds, drawn from the Indian subcontinent and the self-governing Dominions: Australia, New Zealand and later the Union of South Africa, over whom the British high command had no jurisdiction for discipline, training or administration.

The Indian Army made a significant contribution to British forces from the outset of the North African campaign, with the leading elements of 4th Indian Division, initially commanded by Major-General P. G. Scarlett, landing in Egypt in September 1939. This high-quality formation consisted

The Second Australian Imperial Force made an important contribution to the WDF and later Eighth Army. These 'Diggers' belonging to the 9th Australian Division are manning front-line trenches along the outer defensive perimeter of Tobruk in August 1941. (E4791)

The Polish Carpathian Brigade – made up of volunteers who had escaped from occupied Poland and were eager to fight against Nazi Germany – distinguished itself in combat during the latter part of the siege of Tobruk and took part in many of the major actions of the North African campaign. (E8412)

of pre-war British and Indian long-service regulars and a sprinkling of reservists by June 1940. It became arguably the most experienced of all British formations in the theatre, seeing nearly two and a half years of combat, with only a few brief intermissions to rest, re-train and re-organize, by November 1942.

The initial Australian contingent that fought in North Africa landed in Egypt in early 1940. Like other Australian formations of the Second Australian Imperial Force who later served in the Middle East, the 6th Australian Division, initially commanded by Major-General Thomas Blamey, was made up of Australian volunteers who had flocked to join up since 1939 and a handful of regular officers, but initially lacked basic military training, specialized instruction in desert warfare and modern equipment. It was fortunate in having had nearly a year of training, however, before being committed to battle. Their high morale, dash and daring was strikingly demonstrated in January 1941 when the 6th Australian Division, still short of modern equipment, was committed to battle at Bardia. During the ensuing fighting in Cyrenaica its brave, dedicated and enthusiastic officers and men quickly learned their new trade and demonstrated a staunchness in adversity that marked them out as some of the finest troops in Eighth Army. Two further Australian divisions – 7th Australian Division and 9th Australian Division – fought in the Western Desert. Both displayed a similar enthusiasm, with the latter and part of the former distinguishing themselves in action during the siege of Tobruk.

The 2nd New Zealand Division, led by Major-General Bernard Freyberg VC, completed its formation in Egypt in September 1940. This part of the 2nd New Zealand Expeditionary Force was filled primarily by wartime volunteers. It initially fought in Greece and then Crete, where it established a strong fighting reputation, before being committed to the Western Desert where it played a significant part in Operation *Crusader*. It suffered heavy casualties during the retreat to El Alamein and the subsequent pitched battle there, which was particularly serious given the growing manpower crisis in New Zealand.

 THE AUSTRALIAN 'DIGGER'

The Australian 'digger' wore distinctive items of uniform and equipment in North Africa that marked them out from other British Commonwealth troops, although much was later replaced from standard British stocks. The initial uniform worn by Australian troops – a slouch hat (**1**) (with a rising-sun badge (**2**) and unit-colour patch on the puggaree), greatcoat and boots (**3**) – remained largely unchanged since World War I, albeit with the addition of British 1937 webbing and the standard-issue steel helmet as required. The members of the Second Australian Imperial Force also wore distinctive thigh-length four-pocket service tunics (**4**) until these were gradually replaced by British battledress. A rising-sun badge was worn on the collar and an 'Australia' title (**5**) was proudly displayed on shoulder straps. Each soldier also wore Second Australian Imperial Force colour patches (**6**) on their sleeves, with distinctive shapes denoting the formation to which they belonged. This illustration depicts a beaming Australian infantryman of the 6th Australian Division during the early stages of the North African campaign.

The small colony of Rhodesia also made a contribution to Eighth Army, with men serving individually or in small groups in a number of British and South African units. These Rhodesian volunteers undergoing training formed part of the 60th King's Royal Rifle Corps. (E11699)

The Union of South Africa eventually provided two divisions for service in North Africa, built around a small nucleus of its Permanent Force and Active Citizen Force – the 1st and 2nd South African infantry divisions – despite real concerns about the availability of manpower of European descent for the Union Defence Force. Like other Dominion formations it was independent in terms of discipline, training and administration. The 1st South African Division was blooded in East Africa before arriving in Egypt in May 1941. It was soon joined by the 2nd South African Division, as well as armoured-car units. The 1st South African Division was committed to battle during Operation *Crusader*, where it incurred heavy losses. Unfortunately, the 2nd South African Division surrendered at Tobruk in June 1942, with the loss of over 10,000 men. The 1st South African Division fought well at El Alamein, before being withdrawn home to re-form as an armoured formation.

The smaller Allied contingents that fought alongside British Commonwealth troops were very variable in quality, but were all marked by a single-minded determination to kill Germans. The Polish Independent Brigade Group (the Carpathian Brigade), for example, was formed on 12 April 1940 in the Levant. It distinguished itself during the later stages of the siege of Tobruk (August–December 1941). The 1st Free French Brigade, commanded by General Marie Pierre Koenig, played a key role during the battle of Gazala in holding Bir Hacheim against determined Axis assaults.

FIGHTING METHODS, DOCTRINE AND TRAINING

The British Army as an organization knew little about mechanized desert warfare in June 1940, but this had not always been the case. The challenges inherent in living, moving and fighting in the Western Desert had been encountered before when the Light Car Patrols had fought against Senussi tribesmen in 1916–17 along the Egyptian border. Unfortunately, this hard-won knowledge was not officially recorded in terms of written doctrine used to direct operations and training. *Field Service Regulations* (FSR) – the tactical bible of all the British armed forces – discussed desert fighting in only the most general terms.

The early tactics employed by British forces in the Western Desert were pioneered by the Mobile Division, commanded by Major-General Percy Hobart between 1938 and 1939, during intensive training it carried out in Egypt. This taught its troops many of the basic skills required to live, move and fight in desert terrain. Hobart, an outspoken supporter of the RTC and a disciple of J. F. C Fuller, firmly believed that tanks, possessing a deadly combination of firepower, protection and cross-country mobility, were the master of the modern battlefield, capable of winning battles without the support of the other 'outdated' arms of service. The vastness of the Western Desert and low force-to-space ratios meant that the fighting methods taught by Hobart placed a premium on mobility, flexibility and surprise, with small, fast-moving, and widely dispersed columns of light and cruiser tanks manoeuvring virtually at will over wide expanses of desert in search of an open flank or the vulnerable rear of an opponent. However, such dispersion prevented concentration at the decisive place and often involved taking logistical risks. A high standard of desert navigation employing sun compasses, speedometers and maps proved vital to carrying out these tactics, given the vastness of the desert, the absence of landmarks and the poor quality of maps. Basic desert-survival skills were also essential.

The sheer immensity of the desert battlefield and the wide dispersion required to reduce the impact of long-range enemy defensive fire are driven home in this picture of infantry advancing past the wreck of a German Panzer Mk III at El Alamein in October 1942. (E18787)

Hobart's fervent belief in the supremacy of the tank was reflected in the tank-heavy organization of the 7th Armoured Division (fielding some 300 tanks in two brigades), which had very few other supporting arms in comparison. Indeed, a dismissive attitude was displayed towards the 'vulnerable' infantry and artillery, especially anti-tank guns, the role of which was neglected. Indeed, the infantry's role within the division was regarded as extremely limited given the vulnerability of troops on foot or aboard vehicles in daylight unless very widely deployed or dug in. The task of the infantry – just two motorized battalions in an armoured division – was largely confined to protecting leaguers, holding defensive positions or making set-piece attacks at night, assisted by dedicated infantry tanks, against enemy defences. Similarly, the function of the artillery was downplayed given the prevalence of dispersed fleeting targets, poor communications and the lack of an effective British anti-tank gun. This made the use of concentrated artillery fire exceptionally difficult except against pinpointed positions during deliberate attacks.

The early successes enjoyed by the highly trained professionals in the 7th Armoured Division and the 4th Indian Division – making up the WDF at Sidi Barrani and later Beda Fomm – showed that the British quite simply were better trained and fitted to desert fighting in terms of tactics, equipment and organization than their lacklustre Italian opponents. Indeed, the fighting appeared to bear out the tenets laid down in *Field Service Regulations*, especially 'the spirit of mobility, flexibility and the emphasis on surprise' it enshrined. To many officers it fully justified Hobart's view that tanks could win battles by shock, surprise and manoeuvre alone, that wide dispersion was justified and that taking logistical risks paid enormous dividends. A frustration with the infantry's subservient role in the 7th Armoured Division, however, prompted the formation of so-called 'Jock Columns' by the Support Group from 1940 onwards, which were formation consisting of all arms except tanks, intended to attack vulnerable enemy transport.

The limitations of pre-war doctrine and of the lessons learned against Italian troops in 1940, however, were graphically exposed when the WDF was pitted against the German Wehrmacht after the Deutsches Afrika Korps

B **THE LAND MINE**

The land mine – both anti-tank and anti-personnel – initially had little more than nuisance value in the Western Desert, but from the battle of Gazala onwards mines laid in their millions exerted a dominant influence on the battlefield. Initially, however, knowledge of mine clearance was crude in the extreme, with troops using bayonets to prod the ground to locate a suspected minefield. The growing depth, extent and sophistication of Axis minefields meant that the Royal Engineers developed innovative new mine-clearance techniques for gapping minefields, which were standardized throughout Eighth Army during the El Alamein campaign. Mine-clearing equipment included the British Mark IV, 'Goldak' and 'Polish' mine detectors. There were also primitive flail tanks: the 'Scorpion' Mk I was fitted with rotating drums with chains attached that literally beat the ground ahead of the moving tank.

An Eighth Army School of Mine Clearance was established at Burg el Arab to teach the best way of gapping minefields using standardized drills to lift mines and mark gaps. This illustration shows Sikh troops forming part of the 4th Indian Division being introduced to mine-clearance techniques during the period of intensive training before the second battle of El Alamein. Two Royal Engineers are demonstrating the 'Polish' mine detector to the assembled audience. Such training was not without hazard. In early August 1942, for example, a demonstration of mine clearance ended in tragedy when an instructor accidentally detonated a stack of mines amidst his closely packed pupils from the 1/2nd Gurkha Rifles, killing 68 and virtually destroying the headquarters company as an organized sub-unit.

(DAK), led by Generalleutnant Erwin Rommel, landed at Tripoli in February 1941. These experienced and highly professional German troops quickly showed themselves to be superior in tactical doctrine, training and overall combat effectiveness. This small German force threw the British back from Cyrenaica between March and April 1941, besieged Tobruk and then fought the WDF to a standstill on the Egyptian frontier, despite themselves knowing little about desert warfare. Indeed, the 'bad habits' learnt fighting the Italians played directly into German hands. A generally superior approach to combined-arms tactics, overall higher levels of training and arguably better-armoured and more reliable tanks paid the DAK repeated dividends on the battlefield. In particular, the Germans' belief that the towed anti-tank gun was the most effective means of destroying enemy armour was fully vindicated. Unfortunately instead of correctly analysing German fighting methods, most of the British preferred instead to blame defeat on real and imagined problems with their own tanks, anti-tank guns and equipment.

The unpalatable underlying reason for repeated British defeats was the sharp fall in the overall combat effectiveness of the WDF since Beda Fomm, a result of battle casualties and the transfer of experienced troops to other theatres of war. This was a result of the massive expansion of the British Army since 1939, with a huge influx of volunteers and conscripts who knew comparatively little about soldiering. These undertrained and inexperienced inforcements quickly outnumbered the early desert veterans of the 7th Armoured Division, whose tactical methods they copied uncritically. A lengthy period of intensive individual and collective training as units and formations under desert conditions was desperately required to teach them how to live, move and fight in the desert and turn these tyros into soldiers capable of holding their own against Axis troops. Unfortunately time, facilities and opportunity amid the hurly burly of the North African campaign, as well as the requisite fuel, vehicles and equipment, were lacking between 1940 and 1942. Indeed, following Operation *Battleaxe* the new Commander-in-Chief, Middle East, deliberately halted further operations until improvements were made.

An Indian soldier takes the surrender of a dazed German tank crewman, whose Panzer Mk IV has just been knocked out by anti-tank fire. (E3767E)

The first few minutes following surrender were always the most dangerous for prisoners of war, especially if they had been engaged in pitched battle with their captors a few minutes earlier. In this picture New Zealand troops take prisoner the crew of a captured Matilda tank that has been pressed into German service. (E3744E)

The successful results of Operation *Crusader* in November–December 1941 and the ensuing advance to Benghazi were quickly overshadowed by heavy casualties and the German riposte that retook most of Cyrenaica. The many errors committed by Eighth Army showed that its poorly trained troops still had much to learn about adapting to fight a fluid North African campaign against the German Wehrmacht and its rapidly improving Italian allies.

The senior officers and staff at the headquarters of Middle East Command and Eighth Army made serious endeavours to learn from hard-won experience and to disseminate and translate this knowledge into improved training and fighting techniques. Locally produced training pamphlets and training instructions containing new guidance were issued to formations under their command, listing the latest lessons learnt. The key lesson driven home by the *Crusader* battles was the vital necessity of improving combined-arms tactics and both individual and collective training, with senior commanders now fully appreciating that British Commonwealth troops were unable to coordinate tanks, infantry and artillery successfully in either attack or defence. On numerous occasions British armour, for example, had suffered heavy losses charging German anti-tank guns because they lacked the supporting artillery or infantry to suppress them. Eighth Army's headquarters directed early in January 1942 that tanks must never again operate without close artillery support. Similarly, infantry divisions should always cooperate closely with tanks and artillery in the attack, although this was already being practised effectively by many infantry formations working closely with tank brigades equipped with infantry

The Matilda met its match during Operation *Battleaxe* in May–June 1941 after German 88mm anti-aircraft guns were deployed in the defences along the Egyptian frontier, the high-velocity shells of which destroyed the attacking British tanks in a matter of minutes. (E5559)

The Libyan port of Tobruk was subjected to intense air raids and artillery bombardment during its protracted siege in 1941, with its beleaguered garrison finding shelter in its extensive Italian pre-war defences and caves. (E4814)

tanks. Progress in improving combined-arms tactics was impeded, however, by the necessity of employing field artillery in an anti-tank role, a lack of medium artillery and extremely poor communications, which precluded gunners from firing indirect concentrations of any size.

The main conclusion that Auchinleck drew from Operation *Crusader* was that the brigade group was the main manoeuvre and combat element in desert fighting and that improved combined-arms cooperation and tactical flexibility could be achieved only via organizational decentralization. The tank-heavy 7th Armoured Division was accordingly reorganized into one armoured brigade, containing a single infantry battalion in addition to armoured regiments, and a motor brigade of lorried infantry. Other armoured formations followed suit. Each infantry division (except those from the Dominions, who refused) was split into three brigade groups. Each brigade group – whether infantry or armour – was allocated its own artillery and other supporting arms, making it capable of fighting separately if needed, with divisional headquarters theoretically controlling disparate types of brigades as the ever-changing situation demanded.

The linear defensive formation adopted by Eighth Army at Gazala early in 1942 reflected these new organizational changes. It consisted of deep minefields behind which were located a series of essentially static defensive 'boxes' each containing an infantry brigade group whose vulnerable transport had been sent to the rear. Each box was surrounded by a dense minefield and was stocked with food, water and ammunition to last a week. It was intended that the boxes would protect the infantry from enemy tanks and act as pivots of manoeuvre for Eighth Army's armoured reserves when the final strength and direction of an Axis thrust became clear.

The crews of tanks and other vehicles were lucky compared with the ordinary infantryman serving in the Western Desert in being able to carry extra clothing, equipment and personal comforts on campaign in or on the exterior of their vehicles.
 In this picture officers of the 11th Hussars shield themselves from the burning sun with a parasol. (E380)

Unfortunately, the process of reorganizing Eighth Army was still incomplete when Rommel struck in late May 1942. The disastrous Gazala battles that raged between May and June 1942 and the ensuing fall of Tobruk drove home just how shockingly poor British combined-armed tactics on the battlefield remained. Flawed command-and-control arrangements made the British high command slow to react and low levels of training were still apparent throughout Eighth Army. The upshot was a humiliating defeat as the DAK outflanked the Gazala Line from the south and surged into Eighth Army's rear areas. The boxes upon which the defence depended were too far apart to provide mutual support, were deficient in firepower, lacked transport to make good an escape and were in turn destroyed in detail by the concentrated DAK when Eighth Army failed to strike back with its massed armoured reserves in time. The eventual counter-offensive by Eighth Army's armoured divisions fared little better. Each armoured brigade was committed to battle piecemeal without support from other arms or other armoured formations, and each was destroyed in turn. The artillery, in which the British enjoyed a qualitative and 8:5 numerical superiority, was 'penny-packeted' throughout Eighth Army and was never concentrated against important targets.

The early campaigns in the Western Desert yielded the WDF a rich haul of Italian prisoners, whose lack of motor transport made escape impossible when they were cut off by advancing British troops. In this picture, men of the 9th Australian Division at Tobruk take some of the first German prisoners to be captured in North Africa. (E2478)

Eighth Army paid a heavy price for its failure to concentrate its numerically superior tanks, artillery and infantry at the decisive point and time, poor combined-arms tactics and low overall training levels. The inability of the hapless Lieutenant-General Neil Ritchie to grip his command meant that on 25 June General Sir Claude Auchinleck took over the badly battered Eighth Army. A series of further root-and-branch changes in tactical technique and organization, reversing orthodoxy overnight, were quickly implemented by Auchinleck to fit Eighth Army to fight a flexible, mobile defensive battle. He had learned important lessons from the Gazala battles and was determined not to repeat the same mistakes.

The crippling losses suffered by Eighth Army's badly demoralized armoured formations meant that by early July 1942 they were incapable of playing a major part in further fighting until rested, re-formed and re-equipped. The fate that had befallen static boxes and a lack of armour convinced Auchinleck to give his remaining infantry a larger mobile role. All manpower that could not be lifted by the limited available transport was immediately withdrawn, leaving behind a smaller number of fully mobile units to protect the artillery and armour. The remaining formations – organized into ad hoc battle groups containing the maximum number of field guns available and just enough lorried infantry to protect them – were ordered to exploit fully their mobility and provide mutual support to others if attacked.

By far the most important step taken was to reorganize the artillery. Eighth Army effectively rediscovered artillery as a battle winner from June 1942 onwards when Auchinleck decided to concentrate it under divisional, corps and army control, effectively restoring it to its predominant place on the battlefield. Such a major change was made possible by Allied air superiority, the availability of sufficient 6-pdrs to free artillery from its anti-tank role, improvements in command and control and the shortening of the battlefront at Alamein that made it possible to physically concentrate the guns. A combination of these factors improved response times, the weight of concentrations fired in attack and defence and the sophistication of fire plans. As a result, Eighth Army's massed artillery inflicted hammer blows on the DAK in July 1942, effectively halting its advance.

The eventual stabilization of the front line at El Alamein in July 1942, with its flanks anchored on the Mediterranean and the Quattara Depression, clearly vindicated Auchinleck's radical new emphasis on artillery firepower and mobility. His reforms to the organization and fighting methods of Eighth Army, carried out without explanation in the heat of battle, had caused consternation since few of his subordinates understood the rationale for them. This halt gave Eighth Army a breathing space to take stock of the situation and study the recent fighting, which had reinforced old lessons about the need for further improvements in combined-arms tactics and training and for concentrating artillery firepower. A key lesson that Auchinleck drew from the fighting was that a continued lack of cooperation between the infantry and armour required further radical overhauling of the organization of armoured formations. This proved to be widely unpopular amongst his subordinates. To blur the distinction between the arms and to improve cooperation between them he proposed reorganizing every formation in Eighth Army as a 'mobile division', composed of one armoured and two infantry brigades, although the exact composition and balance would depend on an allocated task. New tactical problems, moreover, confronted Eighth Army at El Alamein as the German defences facing it grew in strength, depth and sophistication, using unprecedented quantities of land mines.

The defence of the El Alamein position against an awaited German offensive was not left in Auchinleck's hands. Unlike his predecessor, Lt. Gen. Bernard Montgomery gripped his new command and ruthlessly imposed his personality and his own ideas about organization, fighting methods and training, with the plans and policies of his predecessor forming a firm foundation.

The successful defensive battle against Panzerarmee Afrika at Alam Halfa provided a massive fillip to morale and enabled Montgomery to resist pressure to launch an offensive until Eighth Army was fully ready. The following lengthy pause in operations afforded Eighth Army a breathing space and gave it a badly needed opportunity to rest, reorganize, re-equip and above all for all its troops to carry out the intensive training they so badly needed for the operations to come. In a series of training instructions issued to Eighth Army,

THE ATTACK

The capture of heavily fortified enemy defensive positions, deployed in considerable depth, was arguably the greatest problem facing the Desert Rats during the last stages of the North African campaign, with Axis troops displaying dogged determination in holding their ground despite the overwhelming strength pitted against them. Eighth Army eventually developed a sophisticated technique involving tanks, artillery and infantry working in close cooperation, together with close air support, to breach Axis defences by advancing into them using short and deliberate steps. Engineers played a pivotal role in locating and lifting enemy minefields, creating gaps that allowed the other arms to assault the enemy defences. Infantry and massed artillery played a dominant role in the fighting, with tanks given a supporting role given their inability to break out of minefield gaps on a narrow front in the face of strong anti-tank defences. These combined-arms tactics proved highly effective, wearing down the Axis armies in bitter attritional fighting, but at a heavy cost in casualties.

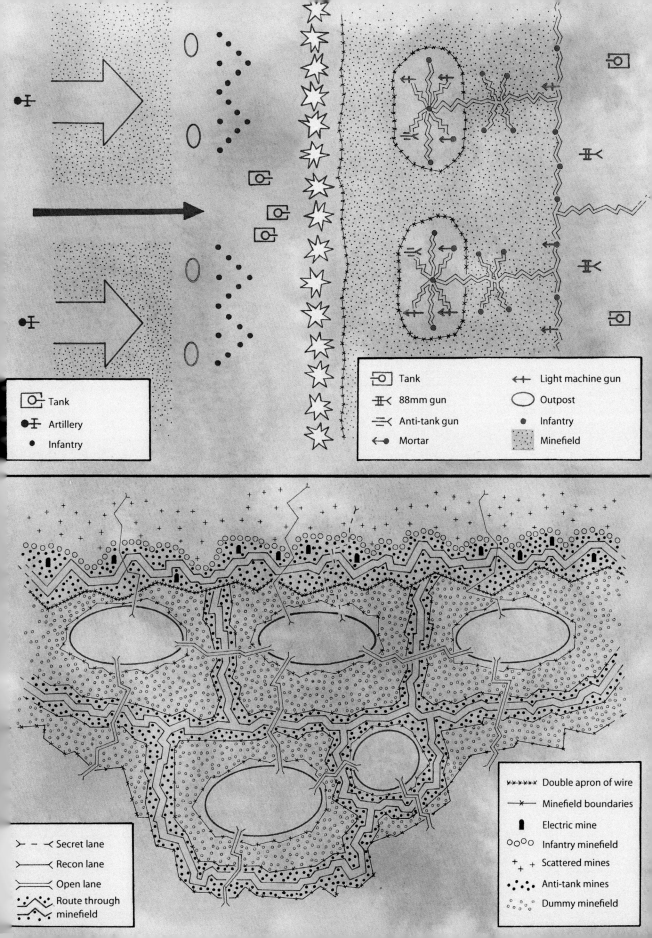

Legend (upper left):
- Tank
- Artillery
- Infantry

Legend (upper right):
- Tank
- 88mm gun
- Anti-tank gun
- Mortar
- Light machine gun
- Outpost
- Infantry
- Minefield

Legend (lower left):
- Secret lane
- Recon lane
- Open lane
- Route through minefield

Legend (lower right):
- Double apron of wire
- Minefield boundaries
- Electric mine
- Infantry minefield
- Scattered mines
- Anti-tank mines
- Dummy minefield

The troops who fought at the second battle of El Alamein came from all over the British Empire, albeit with a growing proportion of troops from the UK. This picture shows four men of the 51st Highland Division dug in near El Alamein on 27 October 1942. (E18625)

BELOW

The carefully dug defensive positions built near El Alamein provided the hard-pressed retreating troops of Eighth Army with a refuge in July 1942. Massed artillery was employed with deadly effect by the British high command to check the Axis advance that had begun at Gazala. (E14575)

BELOW RIGHT

Initially, the anti-tank mine played a small role in the fighting in North Africa, but as the North African campaign progressed minefields of increasing size and complexity were employed by both sides as an antidote to tank attack. (E13905)

the new GOC repeatedly stressed the importance of combined-arms tactics, battle drills, concentration of force at the decisive point and time, the centralization of artillery firepower and the devastating power of close air support on the battlefield. It was to pay a massive dividend for the rest of the North African campaign. Further experimentation with organization was immediately stopped, with Montgomery directing that henceforward divisions would fight as complete formations. The artillery methods developed largely under Auchinleck's command were adopted across the army and further attention was directed towards preparing for breakthrough operations involving the gapping of deep minefields. The steady arrival of long-awaited modern Sherman tanks, artillery and fresh troops, moreover, gave Eighth Army a massive qualitative and numerical advantage over Panzerarmee Afrika, which in comparison was a wasting asset.

The set-piece, largely cautious, old-style attritional battle fought by the 'new' Eighth Army at El Alamein in October–November 1942 effectively ground down Panzerarmee Afrika until it had little option but to withdraw or face complete destruction. Although it had not gone completely to plan, and had involved heavy casualties, this crushing victory clearly demonstrated that British forces in North Africa had by November 1942 acquired a new

confidence. They had attained a high level of tactical and operational skill in fighting a type of battle they understood well, and one that fitted the capabilities and limitations of the troops. Eighth Army had at last developed a 'interlocking system of war' that enabled it to master its desert foe using an astute combination of firepower, fighting skill and careful manoeuvre instead of trying to fight a war of manoeuvre largely on German terms that it had yet to master. This effective, albeit cautious, approach to fighting was employed by a confident and highly effective Eighth Army with deadly effect until the end of the war in North Africa and later in the Mediterranean and North–West Europe.

BELIEF AND BELONGING

The ordinary Desert Rat enjoyed high morale, a fierce sense of self-belief and a real sense of belonging to Eighth Army by May 1943. This had not, however, always been the case. Indeed, the morale of British Commonwealth troops in the Western Desert waxed and waned wildly as the war progressed, reaching its nadir following the battle of Gazala.

The high morale and *esprit de corps* enjoyed by the original Desert Rats serving in the WDF in 1940–41 was a direct result of good leadership, lengthy training before hostilities began, early battlefield success and the fact that its formations were predominantly composed of long-service regulars. The dour General Sir Archibald Wavell and the far more charismatic initial commander of the WDF – Lieutenant-General Richard O'Connor – exerted firm and inspiring leadership over its close-knit regular troops and radiated confidence, integrity and calmness in adversity, while those at lower levels all worked effectively as a team. The high morale of the WDF rested upon other solid foundations, with individual soldiers fighting for their immediate circle of friends, their regiment and to a lesser extent the formation and national contingent to which they belonged.

The ordinary Desert Rat in large part fought for and felt a sense of 'belonging' to his own circle of mates or peer group, with whom he lived and fought. A combination of a shared experience of physical hardship and living at close quarters for long periods of time 'up the Blue' meant that soldiers

The strength and ferocity of the sandstorms encountered in North Africa was an unpleasant surprise to new arrivals, and on occasion they were sufficient to halt all military operations until the sand had settled and vision had improved. (CBM1358)

bonded together and developed a sense of loyalty and a close mutual respect for their immediate officers, NCOs and other ORs, to whom they entrusted their own survival. This feeling of intense loyalty, masculine pride and a resulting desire not to let down one's fellow soldiers always acted as a powerful boost to morale and combat effectiveness as long as a soldier's small band of friends remained intact.

The peculiarly British regimental system, in which units were drawn from a particular regional area and each was intensely proud of its hard-won traditions, beliefs and history, played a significant role in fostering combat morale. A sense of belonging to a regimental family, to which each soldier owed loyalty and whose proud fighting traditions men had to live up to, was carefully instilled during initial training by instructing recruits in their regiment's customs and history and by wearing distinctive headgear, badges, shoulder patches and insignia, which differentiated them from other units.

Those troops coming from the self-governing Dominions already possessed a powerful sense of belonging as a result of their distinct national identities, martial traditions and a desire to prove themselves in battle compared with British troops. This separateness was emphasized by the wearing of distinctive items of uniform and insignia that differentiated them from the British Army. Australian troops sported a national cockade on their slouch hats, for example, as well as shoulder patches identifying their battalion and division.

The confidence and insouciance these early Desert Rats displayed in the face of the shared privations of desert life set the tone of the desert forces and founded a sense of belonging to the only part of the British Army actively striking back at Nazi Germany. A lived-in look and items of distinctive kit worn by veterans was the most visible manifestation of being a Desert Rat, something that was quickly emulated by new arrivals, with officers donning paisley cravats, corduroy slacks and boots of their own. The shared slang used

The ability of individuals and unit cooks to transform quite monotonous rations into a palatable meal played a vital role in keeping up morale. In this picture the crew of a Mk VIB light tank prepare their Christmas dinner in December 1940. (E1501)

by the desert veterans also contributed to a sense of being different.

The high morale displayed by early members of the WDF was not maintained as the North African campaign progressed. The very different traditions, backgrounds and fiercely defended independence of the Dominion and Allied troops militated against effective team-building. Furthermore, the WDF's initial members were outnumbered by mostly inexperienced newcomers to the Western Desert as the size of the force increased. Although the new men rapidly absorbed the ethos and mores of their comrades, their morale proved fragile. Indeed, the majority of these citizen soldiers had little relish for fighting, did not identify with the Army, had hazy notions of the causes for which they were fighting and had not been primed to kill in the same way that their Nazi adversaries had.

The 4th Indian Division played an important part in the North African campaign throughout its duration. These jawans, who have previously served on the North-West Frontier of India, have decorated the side of their truck with the words 'Khyber Pass to Hellfire Pass'. The latter was the nickname for the strategically important Halfaya Pass, which their division unsuccessfully attacked during Operation *Battleaxe*. (E3660)

Eighth Army was formed in September 1941 and initially lacked a sense of corporate identity and strong leadership. Its early commanders – Cunningham and Ritchie – lacked their predecessors' charisma and did not exude confidence. Similarly, Auchinleck, although a calm, courageous and highly professional officer, never satisfactorily imposed his authority. A rapid turnover in its leadership and composition, like the WDF before, meant that Eighth Army lacked an institutional memory. It took a very long time to weld together the various fragments into a coherent whole.

The initial determination and enthusiasm that had marked out many Eighth Army troops before Operation *Crusader* and that had sustained them during the ensuing pitched fighting in Cyrenaica was not maintained. Indeed, it was soon replaced by a growing cynicism, as a shared experience of bitter defeat and constant retreat made serious inroads into Eighth Army's collective morale. This shaken spirit vividly manifested itself in an unhealthy fear of and a respect for Rommel, who was openly regarded by British troops as the best general in North Africa. A haunting fear that victory was forever out of the grasp of Eighth Army spread.

The morale of infantry units suffered hammer blows given their apparent inability to defend themselves against tank attack. A deep-seated mutual mistrust – bordering on hatred – was felt between the infantry and armour, given the perceived failure of the latter to support the former and allegations that the former always demanded support even when it was not required. A combination of crippling losses, perceived shortcomings of their tanks compared with the German Panzers, repeated organizational changes and defeat meant that the confidence, cohesion and *esprit de corps* of British armoured units was badly shaken following Gazala and it became combat-shy for a significant period. A decline in morale in mid-1942 was attributed to the hasty formation of composite units made up of men never given the chance to get to know each other. Indeed, the poor state of overall morale led Auchinleck to request the restoration of the death penalty in June 1942 in order to stem the rising tide of desertion from Eighth Army.

The surviving troops of Eighth Army that took up position at El Alamein were puzzled, confused and dispirited, but morale had not completely broken

The few periods of leave enjoyed by men who fought in North Africa were mostly spent in rest camps or in the many bars, restaurants and brothels in Cairo or Alexandria. Those of a more cultured disposition took advantage of sightseeing tours of the Pyramids and the Sphinx. (E7972)

down. The appointment of Lt. Gen. Bernard Montgomery as GOC Eighth Army in August 1942, moreover, marked a watershed in terms of instilling a new sense of self-belief into Eighth Army. A combination of ordering no retreat, an insistence that divisions would fight as complete formations and a massive influx of new troops and *matériel* had an immediate impact on morale, enabling Montgomery to immediately grip his new command and instil a new drive, energy and sense of purpose. The new GOC, who possessed a gift for public relations and an understanding of the ordinary wartime British soldier, immediately made a deliberately populist appeal to get the best out of those men under his command, building upon the existing ethos of the Desert Army. To combat the 'cult of Rommel' the arguably eccentric Montgomery deliberately created a 'fable' of his own. A combination of his distinctive uniform, personal visits to all formations in Eighth Army and carefully staged pep talks struck a chord with his men and won him the trust and confidence of the ordinary citizen-soldiers making up Eighth Army.

The leadership and sense of purpose that Montgomery provided was complemented by what Eighth Army craved – a series of victories beginning with a defensive success at Alam Halfa that continued until the end of the war in North Africa. It welded the disparate elements of Eighth Army together and gave this formation a strong, coherent identity that it had previously lacked. The Desert Rats serving in Eighth Army quickly regarded themselves as an elite, and were lionized by the popular press, who covered their exploits in

The relief of Tobruk in November 1941 resulted in the capture of large numbers of Italian troops left behind by the retreating Axis, but only after pitched fighting that had tested the newly-formed Eighth Army to its utmost. (E7180)

great detail. By May 1943 the ordinary Desert Rat had high morale and felt a deep sense of belonging to Eighth Army. Success undoubtedly went to its head. Indeed, the post-El Alamein Eighth Army was perhaps understandably arrogant, cocksure and overbearing, especially when confronted with other troops who had not shared the same experience of desert fighting. This was visibly manifested when it came into contact with troops of First Army in Tunisia during the dying days of the North African campaign, towards whom it displayed a markedly patronising attitude.

APPEARANCE AND EQUIPMENT

Uniform and equipment

Because of their disparate backgrounds, the Desert Rats wore a wide variety of headdress, items of uniform and equipment on campaign. A considerable amount of latitude was allowed in concession to the desert climate. A lived-in look and a deep, healthy tan quickly became distinguishing hallmarks of a desert veteran, with a spic-and-span uniform and a pair of white or sunburnt knees differentiating new arrivals from the UK.

The headgear worn on campaign varied enormously, apart from in combat when all wore standard-issue steel helmets. Those worn by British troops at other times included forage caps, balmorals and black berets depending on the unit. An even wider variety of headgear was worn by troops from the Dominions, including Australian slouch hats and South African pith helmets. Many men carried khaki woollen balaclava helmets or cap comforters to wear at night or on patrol.

This headdress was seldom worn unaccompanied by goggles, which shielded drivers' eyes from flying sand and dust, or sunglasses to provide protection from the blazing sun and the intense glare reflected from sand and rocks.

The Western Desert was a land of extremes, alternating between the intense dry heat of the day and the freezing cold of night, when troops donned layers of warm clothing. This image shows troops serving in a rear area warming themselves around a brazier. (E14210)

The fierce winds that blew up out of the desert generated fierce sand and dust storms that made everyday life unpleasant in the extreme. To lessen their impact troops donned goggles and scarves and whenever possible found shelter until they had passed. (E3080)

The choice of clothing worn by Desert Rats in the Western Desert depended largely on the season and often varied between the intense heat of day and the cold of night. Some Dominion units, moreover, had their own distinctive items of kit often dating from World War I. During the blistering heat of summer little more than a regulation-issue Khaki Drill shirt and shorts or long trousers were worn. During the comparative cold of the winter, or at night, troops wrapped up in layers of coats, jumpers, khaki battledress, shirts and other clothing that was gradually peeled away as the sun rose to its zenith. Various scarves were also worn, including the Arab keffiyeh. Locally made and privately bought goatskin Hebron coats were also worn to keep out the cold, in addition to thigh-length, four-button sleeveless leather jerkins. Gaiters or puttees were worn above boots.

The ordinary Desert Rat normally wore 37-pattern webbing and equipment over this 'uniform', into which was crammed side arms, ammunition and other equipment. The basic 'fighting order' worn in the Western Desert consisted of a webbing belt, shoulder straps, ammunition pouches and other assorted attached items. In addition, disposable bandoliers of ammunition were draped around the neck, as well as canvas water containers. A small pack contained mess tins, a 'housewife', food, socks, a pullover, and other assorted personal items.

Footwear worn by Desert Rats normally consisted of standard-issue hobnailed ammunition boots over woollen socks. Australian troops wore distinctive tan boots, whilst Indian troops sometimes wore chaplis (sandals) better suited for moving through hot, soft desert sand. Officers normally wore shoes of their own choice, primarily desert boots affectionately known as 'brothel creepers'.

D THE DESERT RAT

The ordinary Desert Rats normally went into battle in North Africa wearing Khaki Drill tropical dress and at times during colder weather they donned standard-issue battledress. The standard Aertex shirt and Khaki Drill shorts of various patterns proved generally suitable for everyday desert life. Perhaps the least popular item of clothing was dubbed 'Bombay Bloomers'. These three-quarter-length 'shorts' could be worn buttoned up or else down with the bottoms tucked into the top of the socks.

Most clothing and equipment quickly became sun-bleached and white in appearance. Wear and tear of clothing and equipment was always heavy in this harsh theatre of war and opportunities for washing were extremely limited given the shortage of water. A 'housewife', containing a needle and thread, always proved an essential item of equipment for making running repairs.

The representative British soldier shown in this illustration, wearing fighting order, is armed with a Bren gun and is surrounded by items of clothing and equipment worn or carried in the Western Desert. The two men making up each Bren-gun team also carried a spare barrel, replacement parts and other specialist tools for the gun – contained within a webbing carrier and wallet (**1**) as well as large quantities of ammunition. Other items shown are a dust cover for the SMLE rifle (**2**), a pair of yellow-tinted sand goggles (**3**), webbing (**4**), a tin mug (**5**), a gaiter (**6**) and a pair of dusty boots (**7**). The Desert Rat insignia is also shown (**8**).

The Desert Rats wore rank insignia common to that of the rest of the British Commonwealth armies. To differentiate between regiments, a cap badge was worn on headdress, as well as unit shoulder titles. Distinctive unit or formation flashes were sometimes worn on the sleeve or shoulder.

The physical appearance of Desert Rats rapidly deteriorated whilst out on campaign, with uniform, equipment and weapons suffering considerable wear and tear. Clothing, for example, quickly became bleached by the sun. With water in short supply, shaving and washing was a luxury. Most men were grimy and lived caked in dust or encrusted with sand as a result.

Weaponry

The Desert Rats all carried standard British firearms, including .38 revolvers, bolt-action .303 Short Magazine Lee-Enfield (SMLE) rifles, and US .45 Thompson sub-machine guns. Edged weapons included bayonets, various fighting knives and kukris.

The .38 Webley or .38 Enfield Mk 1 Revolver was initially the only side arm issued to officers and tank and vehicle crews, despite its ineffectiveness except at very short range. Some US Colt .45-cal. semi-automatic pistols were later issued.

The tried-and-tested SMLE Rifle Mk III, introduced into British service in 1907, was widely employed. With an effective range of up to 3,000yds (2,750m) this highly accurate, rugged and extremely reliable weapon was probably the finest bolt-action rifle in the world. With a muzzle velocity of 2440fps its .303-cal. round had great stopping power. Although it had only a ten-round magazine, in skilled hands it could fire up to 15 rounds a minute. A sword bayonet was always carried, but it was very seldom used in combat.

The Thompson sub-machine gun or 'Tommy gun', capable of providing a devastating volume of short-range fire and having great stopping power, was normally issued to NCOs and tank crews. Instead of drum magazines, which were prone to jamming, more reliable and lighter 20-round box magazines were employed.

Types of grenade carried included the highly effective No. 36 grenade (the 'Mills Bomb'), the No. 69 concussion grenade and the No. 77 phosphorous grenade, which was normally used to produce smokescreens. Depending on the individual, No. 36 grenades could be thrown a distance of around 25yds (23m).

The simple, robust and highly effective .303 SMLE rifle was the standard infantry weapon used by Desert Rats in North Africa and coped well with the heavy wear and tear inherent in fighting under desert conditions. (E53)

A British soldier surveys abandoned and burning vehicles after an Italian air attack on Tobruk on 12 September 1941. (E5512)

The strengthened EY SMLE rifle provided the infantry with indirect fire support. Fitted with a discharger-cup and firing a ballistite cartridge, these specially adapted rifles fired No. 36 grenades, fitted with 7-second fuses, up to 200yds (183m).

Each platoon carried a single 2in. mortar, which could fire smoke, high-explosive and illumination rounds. This effective and lightweight hand-held weapon, with a range of up to 500yds (455m), consisted of little more than a short tube, a simple firing mechanism and a base plate. It was fired by dropping a round down the barrel with the spade or base plate held firmly against the ground.

The highly effective gas-operated .303 Bren light machine gun provided the main source of fire support at platoon level. Based on a Czech design, this extremely reliable weapon weighed in at 23lbs (10.4kg), had a practical rate of fire of 120rpm and was fitted a bipod for greater accuracy at ranges up to 550yds. With a magazine of 30 rounds, the Bren was normally operated by two men.

The tripod-mounted .303 Vickers medium machine gun provided British Commonwealth infantry battalions with a source of sustained fire support that could be employed in a direct or indirect role. (E1818)

The main source of sustained heavy fire support within each infantry battalion came from the venerable but still highly effective and reliable water-cooled .303 Vickers medium machine gun. The tripod-mounted belt-fed Vickers, served by a two-man crew, could fire up to 500rpm directly or indirectly at ranges of up to 3,000yds, but was extremely heavy at 88½lbs.

The 3in. mortar provided indirect fire support at battalion level, firing smoke and high-explosive rounds. It consisted of a hollow tube with a firing pin at its bottom, a bipod stand and heavy base plate to absorb recoil. With a range of up to 1½ miles it had a maximum rate of fire of 15 rounds per minute when used by a well-trained crew.

The bolt-operated .55-cal. Boys anti-tank rifle, with a five-round magazine, was initially the only anti-tank weapon equipping infantry battalions. Its heavy weight (36lbs) and great length (72in.), coupled with its limited effectiveness against all but the most lightly armoured vehicle and its powerful recoil, made it an unpopular weapon.

The Royal Artillery initially shouldered responsibility for anti-tank defence in the Western Desert. Its gunners manned 2-pdr anti-tank guns, firing a 40mm armour-piercing round, which equipped all anti-tank regiments until early in 1942, when it was issued to infantry units. With an innovative three-legged mounting that could quickly fold down to form a pedestal base, this lightweight towed gun had a very low silhouette and could easily point in any direction. Others were carried 'portee' aboard lorries. With a muzzle velocity of 2,650fps and excellent sights, the gun's armour-piercing round could penetrate 50mm of armour plate at 500yds and 40mm at 1,000yds. Its limitations, however, soon became apparent when used against increasingly better-armoured German tanks.

The far more effective 6-pdr anti-tank gun was issued to Eighth Army in April–May 1942. This long-awaited towed 57mm gun had a split trail and shield to protect its crew. With greater armour penetration than its predecessors (60–140mm at 1,000yds) it could engage German tanks at longer ranges and with a far better chance of achieving a kill. It also fired a high-explosive shell effective against personnel. A handful of 17-pdr guns saw service from February 1943. This heavy, albeit highly effective, towed weapon – mounted on a split trail carriage with a gun shield – proved more than capable of defeating all German tanks in service.

E **WEAPONRY**

The small arms carried by the Desert Rats during the war in North Africa had not been specially developed for use in such harsh climatic conditions. In fact the vast majority were standard tried-and-tested British infantry weapons that had been widely employed in other theatres of war. The simplicity and robustness of the .303 Short Magazine Lee-Enfield rifle (1) and the Bren gun (3) generally stood them in good stead in the Western Desert, coping well with the clogging dust and sand that got everywhere. In comparison others such as the Thompson sub-machine gun (4) jammed easily and required far greater care and maintenance. Grenades (5) were extremely useful for assaulting enemy-held defensive positions and trenches. The .38 revolver (7) was widely carried by officers and vehicle crews, though its effective range was extremely limited. To combat invasive dust, covers were designed for most weapons and troops quickly learnt to apply only thin amounts of oil on moving parts since it attracted small particles of grit. Similar problems affected the standard range of support weapons used by British Commonwealth troops. The heavy, cumbersome and largely ineffective Boys anti-tank rifle (6) was initially the only anti-tank weapon at the disposal of British infantry, and it was universally disliked by those who carried it into battle. Indirect fire support at a platoon level was provided by an SMLE rifle fitted with a grenade discharger cup (2) or else by a 2in. mortar (8). The 3in. mortar and the Vickers medium machine gun provided heavier fire support when required at battalion level. Occasionally, standard-issue infantry weapons were supplemented by captured Italian or German small arms.

The Bren gun was employed in both a ground and an air-defence role during the North African campaign, although its comparatively low rate of fire and 30-round magazine reduced its effectiveness in the latter. (E2502)

The mainstay of British field-artillery regiments throughout the North African campaign was the 25-pdr gun, introduced into service in 1937. The early 25-pdrs used in North Africa were retubed 18-pdrs on an improvised carriage with a range of 11,800yds. The 25-pdr Mk II, introduced into service in late 1941, mounted on a turntable, was far superior and could throw a 25lb shell a distance of 13,400yds and was highly effective against troops caught in the open. The 25-pdr, employed in a direct-fire role, came to be relied upon as the principal and most effective anti-tank weapon in the army's arsenal given the shortcomings of the 2-pdr, although its solid armour-piercing round was only effective at ranges up to 1,200yds. This pressing commitment diverted 25-pdrs away from their true role of giving indirect fire support en masse, and especially in suppressing Axis anti-tank guns and artillery batteries.

The number of heavier artillery pieces was initially extremely limited. Until newly designed weapons went into production, World War I vintage 60-pdr guns, retrofitted with new barrels and pneumatic tyres, filled the breach. The first modern carefully designed 4.5in. guns (capable of firing a 55lb shell up to 20,500yds) were not issued until 1941, and the first 5.5in. guns were issued in May 1942 (capable of firing a 100lb shell up to 16,000yds and a 80lb shell 18,600yds). These were major improvements and the guns were highly effective in a counter-battery role.

Tanks

The British used a wide variety of tanks in the Western Desert that were heavily criticized because of their real and imagined shortcomings compared with the German Panzers. Two distinct classes of tank saw service, intended to perform separate functions on the battlefield: cruiser and infantry. The cruiser tank was designed specifically to fight tanks, being fast-moving and possessing an optimum anti-tank capability, with speed gained at the expense of armoured protection. The far slower and heavily armoured infantry tank was designed to support infantry attacks. Close-support variants of both types of tank were also produced, armed with a 3in. howitzer capable of firing high-explosive and smoke rounds.

The various cruiser tanks employed in the Western Desert shared similar defects. These tanks – the Cruiser Tank Mk 1 (A9), Cruiser Tank Mk II (A10), Cruiser Tank Mk IV and IVA (A13) and later the Cruiser Tank Mk VI (A15), or Crusader I – proved to be weakly armoured, mechanically unreliable and prone to bursting into flames when hit. The A15 Cruiser tank, or Crusader II, arrived in theatre in mid-1941 and was marginally better than its predecessor, having a top speed of 26mph and 40mm of armour. Unfortunately, it also frequently broke down. The greatest defect of all these cruisers was the feeble 2-pdr main gun. Although they could penetrate the turret, sides and rear of all German tanks, the frontal armour was another matter. Lacking a high-explosive round, they were ineffective against soft targets, especially German anti-tank guns. Since they were underpowered it proved extremely difficult to simply up-armour or up-gun them, though a 6-pdr variant – the Crusader III – entered service in mid-1942.

The Desert Rats employed two types of infantry tank, both of which were slow, unreliable and had a very short range. The Matilda II, armed with a 2-pdr gun and a coaxial Besa machine gun, proved highly effective in the early stages of the North African campaign, although unable to fire a high-explosive shell. This tank – with armour plating up to 78mm thick – weighed 26.5 tons and had a maximum speed of 15mph. Until German dual-purpose 88mm anti-aircraft guns were deployed, it was the undisputed queen of the battlefield, being virtually invulnerable. But a very limited radius of action –

just 40 miles – and extremely poor mechanical reliability proved to be serious drawbacks. The Matilda's replacement – the Valentine – possessed armour up to 65mm thick, was armed with a 2-pdr main gun and a coaxial Besa machine gun and a maximum speed of 15mph. It weighed in at 17 tons. Until some 6-pdr variants appeared at the end of the North African campaign, it did not represent a major improvement over its predecessor.

The deployment of better-designed and made American tanks finally gave armoured units a far better fighting chance. The M3 Stuart light tank – christened the 'Honey' by its delighted crews – was fast-moving (capable of 40mph), had a 37mm gun and was mechanically reliable. A major drawback, however, was that its thin armour (1½in.) limited its effectiveness in tank-versus-tank engagements.

The M3 or 'Grant' tank that made its debut in May 1942 was a massive improvement over every tank previously in British service. It had a turret-mounted 37mm gun and a 75mm main gun, mounted in a sponson on the right-hand side of the hull, capable of firing both 14lb armour-piercing and high-explosive rounds. This vehicle at long last gave the RAC a weapon capable of engaging both hostile battle tanks and anti-tank guns. It was capable of penetrating the armour of all German tanks as far out as 850yds. The Grant's frontal armour – up to 2¼in. thick – was proof against the short German 50mm tank gun at 250yds and against the long 50mm at 1,000yds. Although slower and less manoeuvrable than its German counterparts – it weighed 26¾ tons fully loaded – it proved highly effective. A major drawback, however, was that the main armament had a limited traverse and its location low down in the hull prevented the tank from taking up hull-down defensive positions.

The M4 Sherman tank was by far the best tank Eighth Army employed. It had all the same virtues as the Grant in terms of speed (23mph), 75mm armour and great mechanical reliability, but also had the massive advantage

The American-manufactured Grant tank was warmly welcomed by tank crews into British service since it was heavily armoured and its hull-mounted 75mm gun was capable of penetrating the armour of all German tanks in service, as well as firing a high-explosive round. (E13016)

of having its 75mm main armament mounted in a rotating turret alongside a coaxial machine gun. This gave this 29½ ton tank far greater tactical flexibility and meant that it could engage hostile anti-tank guns using high-explosive rounds from the safety of hull-down positions at ranges of up to 2,700yds.

LIFE ON CAMPAIGN IN THE WESTERN DESERT

The life of a Desert Rat was challenging. Each day troops faced extremes of heat and cold, constant thirst, ever-present fatigue and the constant discomfort and mental strain imposed by front-line service. It was often a boring, repetitive and monotonous existence, dominated by routine and lived in very close quarters with other troops, with whom a strong sense of camaraderie in the face of shared hardship quickly developed. Pitched battle with Axis troops was comparatively rare, with long gaps intervening as both sides amassed supplies.

The Western Desert formed the backdrop to everyday life, and was either loved or hated. Whilst initial training helped familiarize troops with desert conditions, the reality was completely unlike what many had expected. A combination of its immensity, emptiness and eerie silence meant that some always found it an oppressive, lonely and quite disorientating place. A deep-seated fear of becoming lost in its vast emptiness gripped many. As one who fought in North Africa described it, '"The Blue" was … a right bastard'. Others found its emptiness, cleanliness and stark unsurpassed natural beauty, especially at sunrise and sunset and at night, particularly appealing.

A soldier stands guard at a lookout post deep in the Western Desert in November 1941. Behind him can be seen a large sangar made of piled rocks. (E6377)

The desert always posed a danger to the careless or unprepared. The intense, unrelenting and desiccating dry heat generated by the desert sun during the summer months dominated life. With little escape from the sun's rays and the glare reflected from the ground, life was extremely unpleasant during daylight hours, with temperatures in the shade rising steadily towards 54 degrees Celcius at midday. Even in the shade temperatures ranged from 28–38 degrees Celcius. This oppressive heat drained men of energy. Until a deep protective tan developed, sunburn was frequent and heatstroke and dehydration were a constant danger. The winter months were arguably the best, with temperatures dropping to a more bearable level and with rainfall common near the Mediterranean coast. A constant annoyance at all times of the year was the all-pervading dust, grit and sand that penetrated into every nook and cranny of the body, clothing and equipment. Thirst was an ever-present companion, with the poor-quality, heavily chlorinated and brackish water normally available always strictly rationed.

The intense sandstorms that frequently blew up in the desert and which often lasted for days were extremely unpleasant. In particular, the debilitating effect of the intensely hot sand-laden Libyan desert wind, or *qibli*, that blew northwards

The absence of vegetation and other cover made the skillful use of camouflage vitally important to conceal tanks and other vehicles from aerial and ground reconnaissance. This Matilda has been carefully hidden in a hide consisting of camouflage netting supported by wooded poles. (E6589)

out of the inner desert, or the similar *khamsin* wind in Egypt, were keenly felt. On occasion sandstorms of considerable ferocity were experienced, with driving grains of sand pricking exposed skin like needles, clogging machinery and stripping paintwork from vehicles. Dust storms frequently occurred along the coastal strip where vehicles had repeatedly churned up the ground surface. Although harmless, they caused considerable discomfort, required troops to don protective clothing, made navigation extremely difficult and compelled vehicles to halt or slow down.

The flies that swarmed in their millions in areas where battle had ebbed or flowed, feeding off abandoned latrines, discarded rubbish, and unburied bodies, were a particularly loathsome feature of daily life. It was difficult to move food from plate to mouth, for example, without it being covered in a crawling mass of insects.

The Western Desert otherwise proved a generally healthy place, although several common ailments afflicted troops. A combination of the heat and an inability to wash meant that suppurating desert sores were common. These irritating and painful ulcers began as a simple skin abrasion and sometimes penetrated as deep as the bone. Dysentery afflicted many, with the disease spread by flies that got onto food and into mouths, eyes and uncovered wounds. A limited diet meant that some suffered from jaundice, digestive problems, scurvy and other skin complaints. Some simply found the alternating cycle of intense heat and bitter cold every 24 hours both physically and mentally draining.

The average day began early for troops on mobile operations, with both sides exploiting the cool before the blistering sun dominated life. A 'stand to' at dawn began the daily ritual as the sun quickly rose over the distant horizon. A pint of piping-hot tea, made using tinned Coronation milk and copious sugar, would be quickly 'brewed up' in a smoke-stained billycan or mess tin, using water boiled over a blazing fire consisting of a petrol tin cut in half and the perforated lower half filled with sand soaked in petrol (dubbed a 'Benghazi cooker'), after men were stood down. A hot breakfast would be prepared collectively by the crew of each vehicle, rifle section or brought up from a cookhouse in the rear.

The food supplied to Desert Rats each day was generally plentiful, but not particularly wholesome or appetizing. Indeed, its sheer monotony was a serious drag on morale. Most was tinned, although onions, lentils, haricot beans and other dried foods were issued. Occasionally fresh bread, vegetables or fruit were supplied.

The end of breakfast was followed by frenetic preparations for the day's march. Each vehicle crew carefully packed its bedding, tarpaulins and any stores used overnight and loaded them aboard vehicles. Radios were hurriedly tuned into nets. Engines were carefully started and warmed up by drivers. Last-minute checks of fuel, oil and water were carried out on each vehicle.

The time of departure from a bivouac largely depended on the tactical situation, although commonly it was delayed until the sun had risen at least 20 degrees or more above the horizon – sufficient to throw a sharp shadow on a sun-compass dial – or until any clouds had cleared.

The tinned and dried rations supplied to British Commonwealth troops during the North African campaign were largely sufficient for requirements but were not always appetizing, especially in the intense heat of the desert. Fresh food was always in short supply. (E6443)

The main body of an all-arms column travelling deep in the Western Desert was led by a vehicle containing its commander and an officer designated as navigator. The navigator, equipped with magnetic and sun compasses, bore the onerous responsibility of guiding and keeping on direct course a fast-moving column, relying on the sun, often-incomplete maps, cairns or numbered barrels placed in the desert, dead reckoning and sun compasses for direction. The formation chosen for a column normally depended on the tactical situation and proximity of the enemy. The majority of Eighth Army columns always travelled in the so-called 'desert formation'. Instead of moving in a long unwieldy column of route that generated intense dust and caused deep ruts in the sand, vehicles moved either widely separated in line abreast or in an inverted 'V' with a 100yd gap between vehicles to improve vision, cut down dust and make movement easier. Even when driving along tracks, vehicles moved on a wide front given that the surface quickly became deeply rutted. Given the limitations and limited availability of radios fitted in vehicles, inter-communications was normally by hand signal or flag if a change in formation was required.

The threat of a chance encounter with Axis forces hung permanently over the heads of all ranks in the forward areas, with strict military precautions being observed at all times. The crew of each vehicle constantly scanned the going ahead, the sky and the distant horizon for telltale signs of enemy forces or marauding aircraft. Most ground combat occurred in the morning or late afternoon, during a 3-hour window when the heat haze had abated and accurate vision and long-range fire was possible. The danger posed by Axis aircraft was constant, however, especially since a moving vehicle normally threw up a dense plume of dust and left behind lasting telltale tyre tracks in the desert sand that could be easily followed by enterprising pilots. If an aircraft was spotted or heard by an air sentry, a column commander was immediately alerted by whistle blasts, toots on the horn or flag signals. A series of pre-arranged drills would then be put into effect. Only when certain that an attack was imminent would vehicles halt or slow down to

The dense clouds of sand and dust thrown up into the air by fast-moving wheeled and tracked vehicles curtailed vision, made driving extremely difficult and made it virtually impossible to conceal the passage of large bodies of fighting troops across the desert. (E974A)

prevent throwing up clouds of dust visible at great distance, with vehicles taking advantage of any available cover. Others simply hared off at maximum speed in all directions to make it difficult for pilots to press home an attack.

The speed of movement and distance travelled each day across the Western Desert very much depended on the type of 'going' over which vehicles travelled and on their drivers' skill. The early morning was the preferred time of day for driving, with the cooler hours used to maximum effect. By 1100hrs during the summer months it would be scorching hot and the glare thrown off the sand would be dazzling for drivers. Over areas of hard-packed sand and gravel, light wheeled vehicles moved at considerable speed – up to 40–50mph at times – with up to 200 miles a day being possible. Tracked vehicles were limited only by their maximum speed. Similarly it was possible to proceed at speed over areas of low dunes as long as the sand was compacted enough to provide good traction. Drivers always had to exercise great care, and their eyes constantly searched the shimmering ground ahead for a good route that would avoid patches of soft sand or rocks. Wear and tear on all vehicles in the desert was heavy. A blown tyre or broken springs, for example, were common when crossing rocky areas. Any immobilized vehicle was left for a repair truck, normally bringing up the rear, to recover if possible.

 A BREW-UP

The campaign in the Western Desert generated an intense camaraderie between British Commonwealth troops that was perhaps unknown in other theatres of war, with men from all over the British Empire thrown together and united in fighting both the desert and their Axis opponents. Although most spoke English, language problems were encountered given the disparate origins of many of its troops. This illustration shows three representative British troops – a British infantryman from a line regiment, a British tank crewman from the Royal Tank Regiment and a Gurkha rifleman – chatting informally sitting around a Benghazi cooker while awaiting the preparation of a welcome cup of hot tea. A mixture of English and Urdu formed the basic medium of communication between Indian and Gurkha troops and other men from the British Commonwealth, with Urdu and other Indian words already part of the vernacular of Eighth Army and the British Army in general, dating from its pre-war service in the subcontinent. The Pashto word 'sangar', for example, commonly used to describe a protective stone wall built up around a defensive position, was derived from service on the North-West Frontier of India.

A 'brew-up' of tea, heavily sweetened with sugar and Coronation tinned milk, always provided a welcome break from the stresses and strains of everyday life. Indeed, it was a morale booster for most Desert Rats, and a valued opportunity to complain about the travails of everyday life in the desert. If they were lucky then the tea was sufficiently strong and sweet to overpower the taste of the heavily chlorinated poor-quality water.

The danger of heavily laden vehicles becoming caught in quicksand, soft sand or salt marsh was ever-present. It was a predicament by dint of training and experience for which all Desert Rats were well prepared. If a tow failed, the first step was always to identify a patch of nearby hard ground. A vehicle was 'unstuck' using various tried-and-tested methods: by partially deflating sand tires to improve traction and by digging troughs between the front and rear wheels, into which a perforated steel sand channel, a device originally developed by the Long Range Desert Group, was laid with its rearmost ends almost underneath the rear tyre. Laying a canvas-and-slatted-wood sand mat in front of each of the front wheels provided further grip. The driver would carefully release the clutch and the vehicle would advance using the traction provided by the sand channels. By the time the rear tyre reached the end of the channel it normally had enough forward momentum to carry it some distance until it reached firm ground. A good push by all the assembled hot, sweating and increasingly exhausted crewmen was also normally essential to provide further momentum. If badly bogged, the vehicle's entire cargo had to be unloaded and then reloaded once it was freed. 'Unsticking' was always back-breaking and exhausting work, especially on hot days. It was a process that often had to be repeated until a vehicle reached firm terrain.

The columns that operated in the Western Desert normally halted when the sun neared its zenith, widely dispersed as protection against air attack, because the short shadow it cast on a sun compass made accurate navigation impossible. The mirages or intense shimmering heat haze at midday also made driving difficult since it was impossible to spot undulations in the ground or patches of soft sand. Mechanical problems with vehicles were also common: sometimes water boiled in vehicle condensers and petrol vapourized in fuel systems. Most troops would shelter from the burning sun under either a vehicle or a tarpaulin stretched out to one side or between vehicles. A Desert Rat would drink sparingly and eat a cold lunch that normally consisted of biscuits covered with spread, tinned processed cheese and oatmeal cake or slices of bread covered in jam (and a fine sprinkling of sand). Drivers refilled with petrol, topped up radiators with water and checked oil levels and tyre pressures. Wireless operators normally listened in for signals, while navigators sometimes carefully followed the progress of the sun using a theodolite as it climbed to the meridian and plotted their current position on a map.

The progress of the column would resume as soon as the sun compass could be used again. As the temperature slowly dropped, life became more bearable again and as much distance as possible would be covered before nightfall. The approach of darkness normally brought travel to a halt, however, as a lack of landmarks and other navigational challenges made movement dangerous except on bright moonlit nights. The ordinary Desert Rat was normally physically exhausted by a combination of long hours out in the burning heat crammed aboard vehicles or inside burningly hot tanks, the stress of being on active service and being caked head to foot with dust mixed with sweat. A period of hard work lay ahead, however, before they could rest.

The consumption of 'exotic' captured German and Italian food, alcohol and tobacco was one of the great perks of the North African campaign, with Italian wine amongst the most prized items liberated from the enemy. (E6509)

The procedure for forming a leaguer was a standard drill. Each encampment was normally square or triangular in shape and organized for all-round defence, with tanks deployed around its perimeter pointing outwards and infantrymen and anti-tank guns taking up position in between. The inner area was normally reserved for vulnerable 'soft-skinned' vehicles that belonged to the infantry, artillery, administrative or support services. The back-breaking digging of slit trenches, gun pits and command posts as protection against air or ground attack was an initial priority for the majority of troops. If the ground was too hard to dig breastworks then sangars would be built up using rocks. Troops normally stood to at dusk, a common time for enemy attacks.

The everyday life of tank crews was physically demanding, with long hours spent each day crammed inside small, hot, airless and noisy compartments followed by working late into the night refuelling, rearming and maintaining their vehicles. (CBM1781)

The men assigned specialist tasks and the crews of vehicles engaged in replenishing and refitting had much work to complete. Upon halting, designated cooks would immediately light a fire, brew up and begin preparing dinner over either a carefully shielded primus stove or a 'Benghazi cooker'. Within 15 minutes each man would have a warm cup of tea to drink, making use of the final pint of water allowed to each of them. An evening ration of a tot of strong service rum, drunk either in the tea or neat, was a highlight of the day for many Desert Rats. Following this welcome refreshment, cooks immediately began preparing a hot supper before darkness fell.

The specialists in each unit were normally kept extremely busy. Signallers erected aerials and established communications. Messages had to be carefully enciphered before being sent, which in itself often took considerable periods of time because of poor reception as a result of atmospheric effects. An exact fix of the location of the bivouac area was another priority, with navigators completing dead-reckoning plots, drawing on their maps the course travelled by the column as recorded using sun-compass bearings and speedometer readings.

The crews of tanks and other vehicles, upon which Desert Rats depended for survival, were always busily employed long into the hours of darkness maintaining their charges, with light from inspection lamps carefully shielded from view by tarpaulins. This included replenishing them with food, water and ammunition and refuelling, with vehicle commanders taking full responsibility for keeping them desert-worthy. It was an onerous responsibility given the heavy wear and tear caused by the penetrating sand and dust. Drivers readjusted loads and checked the mileage, as well as petrol and oil consumption. Other duties included checking engine oil levels, cleaning sand filters and testing tyre pressures after they had cooled off. Gunners would clean all weapons of the sand and grit thrown up during a long day's drive, as well as checking ammunition levels.

ABOVE

The arrival of mail from home was an important fillip to morale for all troops serving in the Western Desert. Few had an opportunity to return home on leave during the course of the North African campaign. (E16270)

ABOVE RIGHT

A permanent shortage of water made washing a luxury for troops serving in the Western Desert apart from a brief 'sponge-off'. To improve personal hygiene and keep cool some troops simply shaved off their hair. (E4758)

The hot evening meal was normally eaten after the sun had gone down in order to avoid the maddening clouds of flies, which vanished by early evening. It normally consisted of a stew, with or without curry powder, made from tinned bully beef or tinned Machonachies meat and vegetables. To this were added dehydrated potatoes or cabbage and bread if available. Other alternatives included herrings in tomato sauce or bully-beef fritters. A crate of hard biscuits was always at hand for those who were still hungry. Official rations were sometimes supplemented by what could be bought from mobile canteens, foraged from the desert or bought from or bartered from Arab Bedouin. Occasionally, captured German or Italian alcohol and food provided a welcome addition to the diet.

The end of the meal marked the end of a day's formal activities for most troops, who could now prepare sleeping quarters beside their vehicles as the temperature plunged and relax as far as possible in the few short hours free before sleep. Many did not enjoy even this brief respite from duty, however, having to return to their allotted tasks. Given their heavy workload, many tank crewmen, for example, did not retire until after midnight, with barely four hours' rest ahead of them before dawn. Most troops slept in narrow slit trenches dug in the sand in the lee of their vehicles, with a tarpaulin providing both a windbreak and a groundsheet.

To keep up soldierly appearances, Desert Rats had occasional haircuts, washed their clothes in petrol and mended those that were torn or damaged. Those needing to defecate took a shovel and walked a short distance out from camp. The pitch darkness of a desert night, however, made this a hazardous undertaking, with a safe return ensured only by keeping vehicles in sight, taking a compass bearing or carefully reeling out a long ball of twine. Others found relaxation in reading, writing letters or simply chatting. Unless a vehicle was running its engine, listening to music on the radio was a comparatively rare luxury deep in the desert given the drain it placed on battery life. A broken night's sleep lay ahead, with each man normally taking a stint on guard duty.

EXPERIENCE OF BATTLE

The battle of the Omars, November 1941

The battle of the Omars formed a small part of Operation *Crusader*, which was launched by Eighth Army in November 1941 and aimed at relieving Tobruk, clearing Cyrenaica and opening up the North African coast. The main thrust was mounted by XXX Corps, commanded by Lieutenant-General Willoughby Norrie, whose armoured troops would swing wide through the desert to defeat the enemy armoured forces outside Tobruk. The latter would sortie out when relieving troops drew near.

A supporting role was given to Lieutenant-General Godwin Austen's XIII Corps, which would pin down the German and Italian troops garrisoning fixed defences at Bardia, Sollum and Halfaya on the Egyptian frontier and others stretching out inland along the frontier wire (demarcating the border between Egypt and Libya), as well as protecting Eighth Army's line of communications. It would then advance northwards towards Tobruk along the coastal strip.

XIII Corps had two infantry divisions at its disposal to carry out its task: the 4th Indian Division, commanded by Major-General Frank Messervy, and the 2nd New Zealand Division, led by Major-General Bernard Freyberg VC, as well as Matilda tanks from the First Army Tank Brigade in support. Its final plan had two distinct elements. The 4th Indian Division would frontally attack and pin down the enemy occupying the frontier defences, while the 2nd New Zealand Division would sidestep them and prevent the garrison escaping northwards. The Axis frontier defences at Bardia, Sollum, Halfaya and farther inland ending up at the Omars were formidable, having been built pre-war and improved since June 1941. The objective chosen for the 4th Indian Division – a formation composed of British and Indian troops – consisted of fortified areas at Libyan Omar and Omar Nuovo, 15 miles south of Fort Capuzzo, and another at Got Adhidiba (alternatively known as the Cova position), located along the frontier wire. The Omars were situated 2 miles apart and Cova was located 5 miles to the north-west. These defensive

The battle of the Omars, fought by British and Indian troops serving side by side in the 4th Indian Division, was a textbook example of how an infantry division could successfully work in close cooperation with a tank brigade in the attack. (E6940)

positions were built around low-lying mounds in the desert that dominated the surrounding plain. Each fortified area was circular in shape, approximately 2 miles in diameter and well supplied. The central humps in each position were heavily fortified with well-sited trenches and gun positions, built in radial groups, hacked out of the rock with mechanical drills and lined with stone. Overhead cover provided protection from field artillery. Most positions were constructed flush with the ground and were so well camouflaged that they were virtually invisible until the occupants opened fire. Belts of barbed wire and minefields encircled each position. These formidable defences were held by the Italian Savona Division, bolstered by small German detachments, for a total of approximately 3,000 troops.

The early days of Operation *Crusader* were largely uneventful for the 4th Indian Division. The 7th Indian Infantry Brigade, the Central India Horse and most of its divisional artillery advanced northwards in a widely dispersed formation along the line of the escarpment, sidestepping the Axis defences, without encountering opposition. The 7th Indian Infantry Brigade quickly crossed the frontier wire and on 19 November took up position north-west of the Omars at Bir bu Deheua-Bir Shefferzen, masking the enemy positions, where it awaited the outcome of XXX Corps' battle. A series of reconnaissance patrols carefully mapped the Axis defences, and armoured cars from the Central India Horse cut communications with enemy troops elsewhere. The 11th Indian Infantry Brigade, meanwhile, occupied the enemy's attention on the coastal sector at Halfaya beneath the escarpment. The 5th Indian Infantry Brigade remained in reserve on the lines of communication awaiting the arrival of troop-carrying vehicles. Further north, the New Zealanders occupied Capuzzo and pushed onwards towards Gambut and the Trigh Capuzzo.

The headquarters of Eighth Army ordered XIII Corps to begin offensive operations late on 20 November, while heavy fighting raged near Sidi Rezegh. The 7th Indian Infantry Brigade, the only part of the 4th Indian Division with sufficient troop-carrying lorries, was given responsibility for attacking the Omars. A single battalion was tasked by Brigadier Harold Briggs to assault each fortified locality, with the 400-man strong 1st Royal Sussex Regiment beginning the operation by attacking Omar Nuovo, which had been identified

The successful attack on the fortified town of Bardia by infantrymen of the 6th Australian Division was the first major battle fought by Australian troops during World War II. It yielded large numbers of Italian prisoners and vast quantities of *matériel*. (E1636)

The lightly armoured Bren Gun Carrier was the 'maid of all work' in infantry battalions during the North African campaign. Its excellent cross-country mobility made it ideal for carrying troops, equipment and supplies up to the front line and for mounting local counter-attacks when required. (E51)

as the keystone of the enemy defences. This experienced British battalion still had a high proportion of regular officers and NCOs, but its ranks were mostly filled by 'hostilities only' soldiers recruited from the towns and countryside of Sussex. If successful, the 4/16th Punjab Regiment would then assault Libyan Omar with the support of infantry tanks. Simultaneously, the 4/11th Sikh Regiment would mask the Cova fortified area before attacking this position at a later date. To the north, the 5th New Zealand Brigade would mask the Axis defences and thereby prevent the defenders' escape or reinforcement.

The attack on the northern face of Omar Nuovo began during the late morning of 22 November with a fierce bombardment by the 1st and 25th field regiments and the 7th Medium Regiment to soften the defences. Overhead, RAF fighters and bombers also attacked the position. To prevent interference with the attack, a smokescreen to blind the Italian artillery at Libyan Omar was laid and at the same time the 4/11th Sikhs demonstrated against Cova from the south.

The assault by 1st Royal Sussex Regiment, commanded by Lieutenant-Colonel Geoffrey Evans, was made at noon by all four of its under-strength infantry companies, mounted aboard Bren Gun Carriers and lorries, with two squadrons of Matilda infantry tanks, part of the 42nd Royal Tank Regiment, in direct support. Unfortunately, the two units had never worked together before. Surprise was lost from the outset when the forming-up area was heavily shelled as the tanks and infantry married up. The fast-moving Bren Gun Carriers led the advance down the gentle and open slope followed by the tanks, with the leading infantry, advancing on a two-company front, loaded aboard lorries moving behind and throwing up clouds of dust. These assault troops were followed by brigade headquarters, the remaining two infantry companies, further tanks and the 4/16th Punjabis, echeloned in depth, all of whom had to cross 3 miles of exposed desert terrain.

Speed was of the essence in order to prevent the enemy from finding a target, with the lorries packed full of anxious infantrymen moving as close as possible to the advancing tanks in order to benefit fully from the latter's ability to keep the enemy's head down. As the advancing troops shook out into a widely dispersed formation the Italian artillery immediately opened fire. To quote one observer: 'As far as the eye could reach the plain was filled with fighting machines speeding to the attack. I had just said "Trafalgar must have been like this" when a whizz and a crash showed the enemy was ranging on us. On the horizon, upright black streaks marked the telescopic ladders of the enemy observers, and we had no hope of concealing ourselves on a plain as flat and bare as a billiard table.' A newly laid Italian minefield quickly claimed four Matildas and three Bren Gun Carriers, but this did not deter the leading vehicles and the infantry advancing on foot closely behind with bayonets fixed . They dashed forwards through the minefield and into the first line of trenches 500yds ahead. Many of the Italian defenders, stunned by the preceding bombardment and the ferocity of the initial rush, emerged from their trenches and strongpoints with arms upraised. A handful of determined Italian and German troops fought on, but within two hours – after the remaining occupied trenches, dugouts and strongpoints were cleared one by one at bayonet point at heavy cost in British dead and wounded – the back of enemy resistance was broken and 1,600 prisoners marched into captivity.

The jawans of the 4/16th Punjab Regiment motored through the wreck of Omar Nuovo while mopping-up was still in progress, and after running into another minefield it deployed 4,000yds east of Libyan Omar during the early afternoon. A fierce bombardment provided cover for its own attack at 1530hrs, with Matilda tanks leading the advance towards a narrow gap located in the enemy minefield. It quickly crossed 4,000yds of exposed desert while shells rained down on the Italian defenders. The gap in the minefield, however, proved to be a carefully prepared trap. A battery of concealed and dug-in German 88mm guns opened up a devastating fire when the lumbering Matildas were within 800yds of the enemy defences. The tanks suffered heavy losses, with the leading squadron shattered by anti-tank fire. As it swung away the second squadron became mired in a minefield, where its stationary tanks made easy targets.

When the 4/16th disembarked for their attack and ran forwards to the first line of trenches only five tanks remained in action. The outer enemy trenches and dugouts in Libyan Omar were quickly cleared at bayonet point as the Punjabis surged through the defenses, carefully outflanking position after position. During the late afternoon steady progress was made as the advancing infantry platoons and sections methodically cleared further trenches, weapon pits and strongpoints. Any points of resistance were outflanked and later winkled out using pocketfuls of captured Italian grenades. By nightfall the Punjabis had penetrated Libyan Omar to a depth of 200yds in the north and half a mile in the south, as well as capturing 500 prisoners, several guns and a large amount of equipment. It proved impossible to clear the entire position completely by nightfall with the limited tank support available, however, since its full extent had been underestimated.

THE INFANTRY ATTACK

The North African campaign has been characterized by many as purely an armoured affair, but it was a conflict also involving many hard-fought infantry actions. The wide-open expanses of the Western Desert, devoid of cover and vegetation, have been described as a 'tactician's dream' by some observers and historians. For the ordinary infantryman serving in Eighth Army, plodding forward across open desert during a deliberate frontal attack on a strongly defended enemy defensive position, it was always a terrifying experience that frequently involved considerable loss of life given the distance at which defenders could open fire. A combination of a lack of cover and Axis skill at camouflaging their positions made careful navigation and wide dispersion for advancing infantry essential, despite the command-and-control difficulties this entailed. The success of an attack was normally dependent on a concentrated artillery barrage and tank support. The latter was normally provided by infantry tanks – the Matilda and Valentine – designed specifically for cooperating with troops on foot. The infantry developed a growing skill for making night attacks.

The wide-open expanses of the desert made wide dispersion on the battlefield and the use of night attacks vital for infantry units in the attack. (E18511)

However, the rapidly deteriorating overall situation near Tobruk on 23 November, where XXX Corps was fought to a standstill near Sidi Rezegh by the DAK, rapidly changed the planned course of the battle. The 'mopping up' of the Omar position was thrown into doubt on 23–24 November when Rommel suddenly disengaged at Sidi Rezegh and launched his 'dash to the wire', with German Panzers surging through Eighth Army's rear areas towards the frontier defences south of the Omars. A state of confusion and virtual paralysis gripped Eighth Army as columns streamed back towards Egypt with troops from both sides becoming closely intermingled across the desert. To meet this unexpected threat, the 4th Indian Division hurriedly abandoned its planned attack on the Cova position, with the 4/11th Sikhs and divisional artillery hurriedly redeployed to protect British supply dumps situated along the frontier wire. The onrush of German armour compelled divisional headquarters and other units to withdraw into the safe haven provided by Omar Nuovo as patrols desperately tried to locate the Axis troops mixed up with the wreck of Eighth Army. The 1st Field Regiment suffered heavily early on the morning of 25 November in a long-range duel, fought in the open desert, with advancing enemy armour, who opened accurate artillery and machine-gun fire from 2,000yds away. The gunners, lying beside their 25-pdrs in the open, finally opened fire at 800yds range and eventually fought off the attack, albeit at the cost of 18 dead and 42 wounded. Their sacrifice saved the 4/11th Sikhs and its transport from being overrun. Further attacks on Omar Nuovo were beaten off by field artillery firing over open sights during the day, although several tanks reached the embattled Axis defenders of Libyan Omar.

Eighth Army clung to its original plan despite the German inroads, with the 2nd New Zealand Division steadily pressing forwards to Tobruk. From noon on 25 November the 4th Indian Division was given responsibility for the frontier area as far west as the line Sidi Azeiz–Bardia, including maintaining New Zealand troops garrisoning Capuzzo and Sollum. The DAK's dash to the wire, however, was over, having had little real effect. On 27 November it withdrew along the Trigh Capuzzo, taking up position in a line from Tobruk through to El Adem and Bir el Gubi, where further fighting raged in a grim battle of attrition.

The 4th Indian Division turned to its allotted task of reducing the frontier defences as the DAK withdrew from the frontier area towards Sidi Rezegh, with the steadily arriving units of the fresh 5th Indian Infantry Brigade providing sufficient manpower to assist with the attack on Libyan Omar. They also freed up New Zealand troops at Sidi Azeiz and blocked all escape routes for the 14,000-strong enemy garrisons occupying Halfaya, Sollum and Bardia.

After reorganizing, the 7th Indian Infantry Brigade made one further effort to take Libyan Omar. Following an intense ten-minute bombardment, the 4/16th Punjabis and 4/11th Sikhs resumed the attack early on 27 November. They advanced 300yds before the leading troops were pinned down, taking several casualties. With dogged determination, the remaining defenders grimly clung on to the southern and western sectors of the position.

The final assault on the position was made by the leading battalion of the 5th Indian Infantry Brigade. It went in at 0515hrs on 29 November, with the 3/1st Punjabis making a surprise attack from the north and the 4/16th Punjabis making a demonstration from the east to occupy the defenders' attention. This night attack did not fare well, however, largely because of the inexperience of the many newly joined recruits in the 3/1st Punjab Regiment (which had suffered heavy casualties in Syria). The attackers penetrated the outer minefield, but as soon as the first defences were reached several men prematurely opened fire. The Axis reaction was swift and devastating. Both leading company commanders were killed, direction was lost in the darkness and most of the attackers were pinned down in the open by machine-gun fire. As dawn rose confusion still reigned, with the attack held up in front of an apparently impregnable position that defied further attempts at infiltration by the leading Indian troops. The 4/16th Punjabis began infiltrating into the position at 1100hrs, but made slow progress in the face of determined enemy resistance. A second attack that afternoon, assisted by three Matildas and 11 Bren Gun Carriers, proved more successful. Two strongpoints quickly fell into Indian hands, and more prisoners were taken.

By nightfall the end was in sight, though 100 German troops still bravely contested possession of the position. These men slipped away during the night, but they were rounded up in the desert by South African armoured cars the following day. The cost of victory had not been light, with the 4/16th Punjabis having suffered 214 officers and men killed and wounded during the eight-day battle. On one day of fighting the 3/1st Punjabis lost 105 men, while the 4/11th Sikhs had lost a further 36. Over 3,000 German and Italian troops garrisoning the Omars had been either killed or captured.

The fall of Libyan Omar marked the end of the battle of the Omars for 4th Indian Division. On 1 December the 5th Indian Infantry Brigade was ordered forwards to join XXX Corps, followed soon after by the rest of the formation, with 2nd South African Division taking over responsibility for the

The Royal Artillery provided 9th Australian Division with vital direct and indirect fire support during the protracted siege of Tobruk. In this picture a 25-pdr gun belonging to the Royal Horse Artillery repels a German attack on the perimeter. (E2887)

frontier areas, whose isolated defenders eventually had little option but to surrender when Rommel withdrew from Cyrenaica. The 4th Indian Division had played a vital part in reducing the Axis frontier defences in November–December 1941, as well as halting Rommel's dash to the wire. Indeed, 4th Indian Division's partial capture of the Omars had denied the raiding Panzers a base from which to draw supplies. The attacks on the Omars had been a textbook example of a successful attack made by an infantry formation in the Western Desert, involving the careful coordination of the three arms of service. A combination of careful planning and close liaison between the 4th Indian Division and the First Army Tank Brigade showed just how powerful and effective well-trained infantry and infantry tanks could be when assaulting well-defended Axis positions.

The 150th Infantry Brigade at Gazala, May 1942

The 150th Infantry Brigade formed part of the 50th (Northumbrian) Division, commanded by Major-General W. H. C. Ramsden, in May 1942. This Territorial division had served in France in 1940 and on garrison duty in England before being sent to the Middle East. The 150th Infantry Brigade served in Eighth Army's rear areas during Operation *Crusader* and its aftermath, during which its training was assisted by the 7th Indian Infantry Brigade and by New Zealand troops. Following a brief stint in Cyprus and Syria, in 1942 the remainder of the formation joined Eighth Army in Cyrenaica early in January, where its men immediately set about learning the ways of the desert.

The 150th Division was deployed as part of XIII Corps, commanded by Lieutenant-General W. H. Gott, in the northern section of the Gazala Line. This linear 50-mile-long defensive position consisted of a deep minefield belt, behind which were constructed a series of fortified 'boxes', each organized for all-round defence and surrounded by minefields and barbed wire. It ran from the coast southwards to Bir Hacheim deep in the desert. This new defensive layout was a deliberate attempt to make the infantry 'tank-proof'. None of the widely separated boxes, however, were mutually supporting. Although the intervening ground was criss-crossed by patrols, allowing many of the men of 150th Infantry Brigade to be 'blooded' in a series of patrol actions carried out by mobile columns operating in no man's land, large parts of the dense minefield belt were not covered by fire. This lack of mutual support was not perceived as a problem, however, since a key element of the defensive plan was that massed armoured reserves would manoeuvre between the boxes.

The battle of Gazala was one of the decisive engagements of the North African campaign and a triumph for Rommel. This picture shows the fighting raging in the distance in the area known as the 'Cauldron' on 9 June 1942. (E13100)

The open expanses of the Western Desert proved ideal for manoeuvring large bodies of armoured fighting vehicles at speed, which could advance and retire long distances with comparative ease as long as they could be supplied with sufficient petrol and other requisites to maintain them in the field. Wear and tear was always heavy. (E18970)

The 150th Infantry Brigade was redeployed early in May from its original well-prepared defensive box to Sidi Muftah farther south. This new position, situated between the Trigh el Abd and Trigh Capuzzo tracks, was incomplete, too big for three infantry battalions and very difficult to defend from the rear. The brigade immediately began improving the position with a will by digging trenches, laying mines and erecting barbed-wire obstacles. It was a hot and exhausting task for its men, still new to life in the Western Desert. Unfortunately, time proved to be in short supply.

The long-anticipated Axis offensive began on the night of 26–27 May 1942, with the DAK, the Italian XX Corpo and the German 90. leichte Afrika-Division leading the advance. This bold attack began well, with the DAK sweeping down past the end of the Gazala Line and then hooking northwards behind the dense minefield belt towards Tobruk, Acroma and El Adem, while the Ariete Division attacked the isolated Free French box at Bir Hacheim. During the initial onslaught, the 3rd Indian Motor Brigade's box was overwhelmed by 21. Panzer-Division and the Italian Ariete Division, the 7th Motor Brigade by the whole of the 90. leichte Afrika-Division, the 4th Armoured Brigade by the 15. Panzer-Division and lastly the 22nd Armoured Brigade by the 15. and 21. Panzer-Divisions. Initially, the British reaction was slow and uncoordinated. A series of unsuccessful piecemeal attacks were launched on 27 May by widely dispersed British armoured brigades as a result, effectively squandering British superiority in tank numbers. By the end of the day the Axis spearheads were deep behind the British front line, despite meeting stronger resistance than anticipated and suffering significant tank losses. The Free French garrison at Bir Hacheim remained defiant while small columns of motorized troops savaged Rommel's long and highly vulnerable lines of communication.

The DAK pressed onwards towards the coast and Tobruk on 28 May, although its armoured spearheads were already running short of fuel and ammunition. Even so, the 21. Panzer-Division advanced past the Knightsbridge Box towards the coast and the 90. leichte Afrika-Division reached El Adem. The 15. Panzer-Division was immobilized, however, by a lack of fuel. Although several supply columns reached Rommel's leading troops, the DAK's overall logistical situation was so critical that Rommel ordered his leading troops to assume a defensive stance. On 29 May the 90. leichte Afrika-Division and Ariete Division began gradually concentrating in a defensive position in a depression 4 miles by 2 miles in area, quickly dubbed by the British the

'Cauldron', lying between the Trigh Capuzzo and Trigh el Abd right in the centre of the Gazala position, with its back to the original deep British minefields. A dense artillery and anti-tank screen was quickly deployed facing westwards while Rommel concentrated on clearing a shorter route for his supply columns through the minefield belt behind him. It was a development warmly welcomed by the British high command, since it offered Eighth Army an ideal opportunity to destroy Rommel's armoured spearheads while they were out of supply, out in the open and penned in by the deep minefields and the defensive box occupied by the 150th Infantry Brigade, whose existence German intelligence had completely missed.

The 150th Infantry Brigade had initially escaped the full fury of the German offensive inside its fortified box, with its attention occupied by diversionary attacks mounted in the Gazala–Sidi Muftah area by Gruppe Cruwell and by shelling and Stuka dive-bombing raids. This pressure gradually intensified, however, as the Italian Brescia Division nosed forward along the Trigh Capuzzo and Trigh el Abd and began gapping the undefended minefield lying between the 69th Infantry Brigade and the 150th Infantry Brigade, effectively isolating the formation from its parent division. Similar progress was made by the motorized Trieste Division in gapping the minefields to the south of the box. Attempts by the 150th Infantry Brigade to interfere were only partially successful. On 27 May the 4th East Yorkshire Regiment, occupying defensive positions covering the Trigh el Abd, for example, successfully destroyed 13 Italian tanks. A shortage, of artillery ammunition – each 25-pdr was rationed to 25 rounds per day – made it difficult to halt the work of the Italian engineers. For most troops in the box little could be done other than listen to the increasing noise of fighting to their rear.

The growing threat from the DAK within the 'Cauldron', and the fact that the 4th East Yorkshires were badly overextended, made an increasingly anxious Brigadier J. C Haydon radically rethink his defensive dispositions late on 28 May. To meet the growing threat from his rear, shallow new minefields were hurriedly laid and slit trenches and gun positions were dug on the eastern side of the box, as the brigade reorganized for all-round defence. During the night the 4th East Yorkshire Regiment withdrew into the box, where it deployed its two companies on the eastern side of the perimeter, with one on either side of the 232nd Field Company, Royal Engineers. The 72nd Field Regiment and a battery of anti-tank guns were placed in support, with its 25-pdrs and a battery of newly-arrived 6-pdrs carefully sited in an anti-tank role. The defensive strength of the box at Sidi Muftah was massively augmented on 28–29 May when the Divisional Mobile Reserve – consisting of the tactical headquarters of the First Army Tank Brigade, commanded by Brigadier O'Carroll, and accompanied by the 44th Royal Tank Regiment and one squadron of the 42nd Royal Tank Regiment – withdrew into the box with 30 Matilda tanks.

The 'fog of war' cloaking the Gazala battlefield meant that the German high command only discovered the size and full extent of the 150th Infantry Brigade's heavily fortified position early on 30 May, when strong DAK detachments bumped into it by accident. It was an extremely serious discovery, since the box dominated the two existing gaps in the minefield with artillery fire and made large-scale resupply impossible except at night. The 150th Infantry Brigade had to be defeated and defeated quickly, while the anti-tank screen dealt with British armoured counter-attacks from the east.

The nervous, outnumbered and already weakened 150th Infantry Brigade was quickly subjected to probing attacks, and the brigade reserve was moved onto the perimeter to the right of the 4th Green Howards. Aggressive patrolling by the British infantry yielded results, with heavy casualties inflicted on an enemy working party by one patrol. On the morning of 30 May, German engineers began lifting the hastily laid minefields on the eastern side of the box, which were a pale imitation of those to the west. An assault by German motorized infantry from the 15. Panzer-Division gained some ground, but these positions were successfully counter-attacked throughout the remainder of day by the Matildas, which successfully plugged the gaps opened in the defences. Panzer-Regiment 5 lost 11 tanks in the initial exchange of fire. A position occupied by 232nd Company Royal Engineers on the eastern face of the defences was overrun during a determined infantry assault, however, giving the enemy a vantage point overlooking a great part of the box. Efforts to dislodge them by combined infantry and tank attacks failed, despite large quantities of precious ammunition being expended. Attacks on the carefully dug-in 4th Green Howards were defeated, and heavy Axis casualties were inflicted during a counter-attack carried out by the battalion's Bren Gun Carriers. As darkness fell, aggressive patrolling immediately began all along the perimeter to prevent further German infiltration across the new minefields into the box.

The eventual fate of the beleaguered 150th Infantry Brigade, if left unsupported under concentrated armoured attack, was never in doubt to all those who served at Sidi Muftah. Unfortunately, it received little of the promised aid as the noose gradually tightened around its position, apart from periodic 'stirring' messages from divisional headquarters and the British high command. Efforts to resupply it with ammunition proved abortive. Although two small diversionary armoured attacks were mounted at Bir Aslagh Ridge and in the Bir Hamat area, they had little impact on the German anti-tank screen. Similarly, a small sortie made from the Knightsbridge Box along the Trigh Cappuzzo was badly mauled by the 21. Panzer-Division. Although plans were put in train by the hesitant and indecisive British high command for further infantry attacks on 31 May and 1 June and a larger armoured counter-attack, it proved to be too little and too late.

The construction of defensive positions in the Western Desert was always a hot, sweaty and back-breaking task for ordinary Desert Rats, with explosives and pneumatic drills required in many areas where bedrock lay just below the surface. If it proved impossible to excavate trenches or gun pits then sangars – walls of rocks and boulders – provided cover. (E13924)

New Zealand troops watching 2-pdr anti-tank guns in action against German tanks on 3 December 1941. The 2-pdr gun provided the mainstay of British anti-tank defence for much of the North African campaign. It initially proved highly effective, but as the armour of German and Italian tanks increased in thickness this 'pernicious little pop-gun', as it was dubbed by one senior officer, became obsolete. (E3745E)

The full fury of the DAK descended upon 150th Infantry Brigade on 31 May, after elements of the 90. leichte Afrika-Division and the Trieste Division deployed overnight around the perimeter. A formal request for surrender by Rommel preceded the initial attack, but was dismissed out of hand by Brigadier Haydon. A heavy bombardment heralded the first assault, with German infantry from the 90. leichte Afrika-Division moving up close behind the barrage. Little progress was made, however, despite a furious exchange of close-range fire in the face of skilful and stubborn resistance by the defenders, and the attackers withdrew at 0800hrs having suffered heavy losses. A German attack supported by tanks on the north-east corner of the box, which was held by the 4th East Yorkshire Regiment, proved more successful and penetrated the outer defences of the box, despite desperate resistance from the 6-pdrs, Bofors guns and infantry that continued until 1600hrs. This penetration was successfully sealed off, however, by the handful of remaining Matildas. The steady destruction or capture of the 6-pdr, 2-pdr and assorted captured Axis anti-tank guns pressed into British service and their crews, however, undermined the brigade's ability to defend itself against tank attack. Heavy attacks were made on the south-east corner of the box at the vulnerable junction between the 4th East Yorkshire Regiment and the 5th Green Howards, where the Germans took ground and prisoners, but the gap opened in the defences was quickly sealed by a counter-attack launched by the headquarters of the 4th East Yorkshire Regiment. The 4th Green Howards also beat off an assault on its sector. A heavy price, however, was paid in dead and wounded by the defenders for these local successes. By nightfall most anti-tank guns had been destroyed, ammunition supplies had dwindled alarmingly and all available reserves had been committed. Only 13 Matildas still remained operational, along with six medium guns, with 20 rounds each, and 12 25-pdrs with less than 100 rounds all told. No support was forthcoming from outside the box. Both sides drew apart as darkness shrouded the position.

The writing was clearly on the wall for the exhausted and increasingly desperate survivors of the 150th Infantry Brigade, whose defensive box had contracted to half its original size under heavy German pressure. The DAK was ordered by Rommel to end British resistance at Sidi Muftah once and for all by bringing to bear all its strength, and to do so it had been resupplied overnight using the nearby gaps through the minefield. Early on 1 June the box was subjected to intense shelling and dive-bombing by Ju87 Stukas, following which the assault from all sides redoubled, with the attackers reinforced by more artillery and part of the 21. Panzer-Division. A series of concentric attacks employing massed tanks and infantry began, which lasted into the late afternoon and steadily wore down the remaining British troops. Although every remaining trench, dugout and gun position was bitterly contested in fierce hand-to-hand fighting by the remaining tough Northumbrian infantrymen, the box was overrun. Casualties rapidly mounted, including Brigadier Haydon, who was killed by shellfire. This bitter fighting also taxed the morale of the attackers, with Rommel personally taking charge of a faltering lead infantry platoon. A German report stated: 'The encircled enemy, supported by numerous infantry tanks, resisted stubbornly. Each separate point within the fortress-like, strengthened defences had to be fought for. The positions had to be taken in hand-to-hand fighting for each individual bunker... The enemy suffered extraordinarily heavy bloody losses.' By late afternoon, as water and ammunition ran out, further organized resistance was impossible and the survivors of the 150th Infantry Brigade emerged from their slit-trenches and bunkers with their hands in the air and capitulated after destroying their remaining guns and small arms.

The 3,000 exhausted British troops who marched into captivity on 1 June had displayed considerable courage, self-sacrifice and dogged determination during intense close-quarter infantry combat despite clearly being massively outnumbered and out-gunned from the beginning of the engagement. Such bravery proved to be of no avail, however, in the face of the DAK's concentrated armoured units. Ultimately, this hard-fought defensive action had proved to be another classic demonstration of the inherent weakness of the Gazala Line and of the static infantry box as a defensive tactic in the Western Desert. The wide gap between the 150th Infantry Brigade and neighbouring boxes ensured that no external support from these sources was possible and as a result its vulnerable, out-gunned and immobile garrison had been overwhelmed. The failure to mount a strong, well-coordinated armoured counter-attack, upon which the Gazala defences depended, effectively sealed the fate of 150th Infantry Brigade as soon as the DAK turned its full weight against it.

The time won by the brigade's extremely gallant defence and the opportunity the situation had offered to inflict a decisive defeat on the DAK was ill-used by the British high command, who failed to mount a decisive armoured counter-attack while the concentrated German armoured spearheads were at their most vulnerable as they were penned within the Cauldron. It was a turning point of the battle of Gazala and arguably one of the greatest lost

The Desert war was characterized by Rommel as a 'war without hatred'. Both sides strictly obeyed international conventions about the care of the wounded and the treatment of prisoners of war. In this picture a captured German doctor assists British medical personnel treating another wounded German prisoner. (E6794)

opportunities of the North African campaign. In comparison, the Axis high command acted with commendable vigour by immediately opening a supply line through the minefield belt and restocking its armoured troops with water, fuel and ammunition. The revitalized DAK, occupying a salient deep in the heart of Eighth Army behind the Gazala defences, husbanded its strength and calmly awaited developments. The badly botched British counter-attack on 4–5 June that had taken so long to organize proved a damp squib that cost Eighth Army another 200 tanks, four artillery regiments and an infantry brigade.

The initiative had now firmly passed to Panzergruppe Afrika. On the afternoon of 5 June the DAK and the Italian Ariete Division attacked the now much-reduced British formations opposing them, with 21. Panzer-Division quickly advancing towards the Knightsbridge Box, while 15. Panzer-Division swung round through Bir el Hamat in another outflanking manoeuvre. Unable to offer effective resistance, the demoralized Eighth Army struggled to prevent the Gazala defences from being overwhelmed. The box at Bir Hacheim was attacked in strength from 2 June onwards by the redeployed Axis troops. It finally fell on 10 June, effectively ending the Gazala battles, although 2,700 Free French successfully escaped. The freed-up German forces quickly moved northwards, adding their weight to the main Axis attacks that inflicted heavy tank losses and eventually ended with the fall of Tobruk and the withdrawal of Eighth Army to El Alamein.

AFTERMATH

The Desert Rats who served in the arid wastes of the Western Desert between June 1940 and May 1943 all displayed considerable courage and powers of endurance. This challenging and hard-fought campaign, with its widely fluctuating fortunes as fighting ebbed and flowed backwards and forwards along the Mediterranean coast, proved a harsh testing ground for troops drawn from all over the far-flung British Empire. It was distinctive in many respects, with all British Commonwealth troops having to adapt successfully and learn to live, move and fight the enemy under harsh climatic and physical conditions. Many paid the ultimate price – approximately 200,000 British casualties were suffered in North Africa (mostly by Eighth Army and its predecessors) – in a series of pitched battles against brave, determined and highly professional Axis troops fighting under arguably the best German general of World War II. For a large number of psychologically damaged and badly wounded Desert Rats the war was over, with long periods of rest and recuperation in hospitals lying ahead. Many were left permanently maimed or mentally scarred by the experience.

The war in North Africa always had particular significance for the UK, with it being for three years the single most important land campaign the British Empire was fighting and the only opportunity to strike back against the might of Nazi Germany and its allies on land. It was by no means an easy experience, with the WDF and Eighth Army suffering a series of humiliating defeats at Axis hands. The crushing victory at the second battle of El Alamein and the pursuit to the borders of Tunisia, however, finally demonstrated to the world that the UK was capable of winning a major battle against the Axis powers. Indeed, it was arguably the last great victory won by the British Commonwealth armies during World War II, establishing a tradition of success and a belief amongst British Commonwealth troops and the civilian

population that they could and would defeat their German opponents. The justifiably proud and elated members of Eighth Army capped their dramatic victory at El Alamein in May 1943 when the last Axis troops surrendered at Cap Bon. Although the final victory went to the British First Army, it was fitting that it contained for the final 'kill' two formations transferred from Montgomery's command that had begun life in the desert, while Eighth Army exerted pressure from the Enfidaville position. The veteran 11th Hussars, part of the 7th Armoured Division, were the amongst the first Allied troops to enter Tunis on 7 May 1943, while the 4th Indian Division took Generaloberst Arnim prisoner on 12 May 1943.

The wartime career of the Eighth Army was far from over, as preparations for attacking the underbelly of Fortress Europe got under way. It was a different army, however, from the one that had fought at El Alamein. Indeed, the winning multinational team of Eighth Army began breaking up soon after the second battle of El Alamein, with the dispatch of the 9th Australian Division to the Far East and the return of the 1st South African Division home. Other metropolitan UK formations were broken up as the British Army was gripped by a gathering manpower crisis that hamstrung the UK's war effort until the end of the war.

A proud, self-confident and highly professional Eighth Army was committed to battle again during the invasion of Sicily. It went on, initially commanded by Lt. Gen. Montgomery and then by Lieutenant-General Sir Oliver Leese, to fight the remainder of the war in Italy, retaining under its command a noteworthy proportion of British, New Zealander and Indian veterans from the Western Desert campaign. A significant number of formations composed of combat-hardened desert veterans, however, were at Montgomery's insistence provided to 21st Army Group for D-Day. The 7th Armoured Division, for example, still proudly displaying the jerboa patch on its pennants, vehicles and newly issued shoulder patches, was amongst those who served in North-West Europe. The fighting record of these formations, however, was mixed in Normandy, with many proving 'sticky' and less inclined to take risks than those who had not yet been blooded in combat.

Photographs of long, snaking lines of Italian and German prisoners marching into captivity escorted by a handful of British guards are some of the most enduring images of the North African campaign. (E6785)

The experience Eighth Army gained in the Western Desert had wider significance and played a pivotal role in improving the overall combat effectiveness of the British Army during World War II. It provided a vital proving ground for troops, and a testing ground for organization, equipment and training. Eighth Army mastered many new lessons about modern warfare during the fighting in the great 'sand table' of the Western Desert. However, it took a long time to learn from painful experience the right lessons about waging armoured warfare under desert conditions.

Indeed, the desert had taught the massively expanded wartime British Army much about waging warfare under modern conditions, especially the handling of large armoured formations, combined-arms tactics and the employment of massed artillery in support of the infantry when making set-piece attacks. As David French has recently observed, the Eighth Army did not copy German fighting methods, but instead found a distinctly British approach to war, relying on firepower, fighting skill and careful movement rather than risky manoeuvre.

The lessons learnt by Eighth Army were not forgotten and were passed on to the rest of the British Army, incorporated in a long series of training instructions, pamphlets and memoranda. A combination of cross posting of personnel, as well as the transfer of complete units and formations, meant that all British regular units and formations profited from the hard-won experience of the campaign in the Western Desert. Indeed, by 1944–45 British forces in Italy and those in North-West Europe serving as part of 21st Army Group and in the Italian peninsula were employing massed artillery and close air support on a hitherto unprecedented scale, in large part based upon methods developed by Montgomery and Eighth Army during the closing phases of the desert campaign.

The vast majority of British infantry units were fully motorized by the end of the North African campaign, although shortages of troop-carrying vehicles were marked during its early phases and this restricted the employment of some formations in battle. (E11676)

H ADVANCED DRESSING STATION

The campaign in the Western Desert was remarkable in the degree to which the opposing combatant troops displayed considerable respect and indeed chivalry towards each other. To use Rommel's own words, it was a 'war without hatred'. Similarly, Generalleutnant Johann von Ravenstein described it as a 'gentleman's war' with very few instances of atrocities committed by troops of either side. The fact that troops of both sides were initially long-service professionals – and that in a way they found a common enemy in the desert itself, with troops suffering alike from the heat, thirst, dust, flies and the harsh desert terrain – may have played a part in maintaining standards of behaviour in accordance with international standards.

The restraint shown by both sides was particularly evident in the treatment meted out to prisoners of war. On numerous occasions advanced dressing stations and forward hospitals, for example, were overrun by fast-moving armoured units ranging deep across the desert, which largely left them strictly alone apart from a cursory check for weapons and combatant troops. Following the terms of the Geneva Convention, British and German medical officers treated prisoners of war on exactly the same basis as their own men. This illustration depicts a shell-shocked and obviously badly dazed German soldier being treated by British medical personnel at an advanced dressing station deep in the Libyan Desert.

The war fought in the Western Desert will always occupy a special place in the history of the British Army, although in the final analysis it was a sideshow, with the defeat of Nazi Germany ultimately determined in the Soviet Union and the fighting in North-West Europe. This perhaps unpalatable truth should not detract from the bravery, self-sacrifice and commitment of those who fought in the Western Desert. These men undoubtedly deserve the kudos, esteem and respect paid to them given what they achieved in personal terms in surmounting the physical difficulties of living, moving and fighting in the desert and winning this hard-fought campaign. It is perhaps fortunate that the best traditions of Eighth Army live on to the present day in the British Army. The jerboa flash and the nickname 'Desert Rats' was still worn with pride by the men of the 7th Armoured Brigade in recent campaigns in Iraq and Afghanistan.

MUSEUMS AND COLLECTIONS

The main archival repository for original documents relating to the Desert Rats in North Africa can be found in the National Archives at Kew in London. These include papers relating to the conduct of operations and changes in organization and planning, as well as war diaries and similar documents relating to individual formations and units, which are perhaps of greater interest to the general public. A caveat should be added about the war diaries, however, since they vary greatly in coverage and quality and often the original documents contained in appendices to each monthly report were either not forwarded to the UK or else have gone missing. Most war diaries were written by overworked intelligence officers or similar, who seldom had time on campaign to produce a definitive account of their unit's activities.

The main source of information elsewhere is the Imperial War Museum at Lambeth in London, which has a large collection of eyewitness accounts and personal papers left by participants in the North African campaign. By far the most important are the papers of Field Marshal Bernard Law Montgomery, which contain a wealth of information about his life and career, including many documents relating to the organizing and training of Eighth Army following his assumption of command. The National Army Museum in Chelsea also has relevant material, including many personal memoirs, and has periodic displays relating to the Desert Rats.

The availability of Desert Rat ephemera with good provenance for collectors is limited. A wide range of headgear, items of uniform and equipment of the type worn by the Desert Rats can be purchased from militaria dealers, though little of that available was probably worn in combat. Insignia – formation signs and regimental badges – are perhaps the most widely available of items relating to the Desert Rats, but should be treated with caution given the large number of fakes on the market. Similarly, the regrettable decision to issue campaign medals without naming the recipient means that medals attributed to Desert Rats, apart from those awarded to South African and some Indian troops, should be treated with considerable circumspection unless accompanied by supporting paperwork.

SELECT BIBLIOGRAPHY

Barr, Niall, *The Pendulum of War: The Three Battles of El Alamein*, London: Jonathan Cape, 2004

Bidwell, Shelford and Graham, Dominic, *Firepower: British Army Weapons and Theories of War 1904–1945*, London: George Allen & Unwin, 1985

Carver, Michael, *El Alamein*, London, Batsford, 1962

——, *Tobruk*, London: Batsford, 1964

——, *Dilemmas of the Desert Campaign*, London: Batsford, 1986

Clay, Major E., *The Path of the 50th: The Story of 50th (Northumbrian) Division*, Aldershot: Gale and Polden, 1950

Connell, John, *Auchinleck*, London: Cassell, 1959

Doherty Richard, *A Noble Crusade. The History of Eighth Army 1941 to 1945*, London: Spellmount, 1999

Ford, Ken, *El Alamein 1942 The Turning of the Tide*, Oxford: Osprey, 2005

Fraser, David, *And We Shall Shock Them*, London: BCA, 1983

French, David, *Raising Churchill's Army: The British Army and the War against Germany 1919–1945*, Oxford: OUP, 2000

Grant, Adrian (ed.), *The Imperial War Museum Book of the War in the Desert*, London: BCA, 1992

Griffith, Paddy, 'British Armoured Warfare in the Western Desert, 1940–43' in Harris, J. P. and Toase, F. H., *Armoured Warfare*, London: BT Batsford, 1990

——, *World War II Desert Tactics*, Oxford: Osprey, 2008

Harrison Place, Tim, *Military Training in the British Army, 1940–44: From Dunkirk to D-Day*, London: Frank Cass, 2000

Jackson, W. G. F., *The North African Campaign 1940–43*, London: BT Batsford, 1975

Latimer, Jon, *Operation Compass: Wavell's Whirlwind Offensive*, Oxford: Osprey, 2000

——, *Tobruk 1941*, Oxford: Osprey, 2001

Parkinson, Roger, *The War in the Desert*, London: BCA, 1967

Perrett, Bryan, *Wavell's Offensive*, London: Ian Allen, 1979

Pitt, Barrie, *The Crucible of War: Wavell's Command*, London: Cassell, 2001

——, *The Crucible of War: Auchinleck's Command*, London: Cassell, 2001

——, *The Crucible of War: Montgomery and Alamein*, London: Cassell, 2001

Playfair, Major-General I. S. O. et al., *The Mediterranean and the Middle East. Volume I: The Early Successes against Italy*, London: HMSO, 1954

——, *The Mediterranean and the Middle East. Volume II: 'The Germans come to the Help of their Ally'*, London: HMSO, 1956

——, *The Mediterranean and the Middle East. Volume III: British Fortunes reach their Lowest Ebb*, London: HMSO, 1960

——, *The Mediterranean and the Middle East. Volume IV: The Destruction of the Axis Forces in Africa*, London: HMSO, 1966

Stevens, Lieutenant-Colonel G. R., *The Fourth Indian Division*, Toronto: Mclaren, n.d.

Stewart, Adrian, *The Early Battles of the Eighth Army: Crusader to the Alamein Line*, London: Pen & Sword, 2002

——, *The Eighth Army's Greatest Victories: Alam Halfa to Tunis, 1942–43*, London: Pen & Sword, 1999

Tuker, Lieutenant-General Sir Francis, *Approach to Battle: A Commentary Eighth Army, November 1941 to May 1943*, London: Cassell, 1963

Wilkinson-Latham, John, *Montgomery's Desert Army*, Oxford: Osprey, 1977

Windrow, Martin, *Rommel's Desert Army*, Oxford: Osprey, 1976

INDEX

References to illustrations are shown in **bold**.